FERGUSON

Ian Allan
PUBLISHING

First published 2001

ISBN 0 7110 2826 5

© Allan T. Condie 2001

Design concept and layout
© Stephen Thompson Associates 2001

Published by Ian Allan Publishing
an imprint of Ian Allan Publishing Ltd, Hersham,
Surrey KT12 4RG.
Printed by Ian Allan Printing Ltd, Hersham,
Surrey KT12 4RG.

Code: 0111/2

Title page photograph:
Alpha and Omega, the Ferguson Brown type A of
1937 with the largest Massey Ferguson tractor of
the 1970s, the 1100.

Photograph on the opposite page:
A Massey Ferguson 65 working with an MF Pickup
baler.

CONTENTS

INTRODUCTION

A Perthshire threshing scene with a Fergie 20 bringing in the sheaves. The Scots called their threshing machines 'mills'.

The twentieth century saw immense change not only in our towns and cities, but in the countryside. The invention of the internal combustion engine and its application to motor vehicles has probably engineered most of the economic and social changes in the second part of that century. If one were able to visit the same farm in 1900, 1950, and today the changes would be incredible. Indeed a visit to any farm in 2001 would see mechanisation in most aspects of activity. Sophisticated tractors with state of the art technology and many creature comforts for the operator effortlessly plough and till the land. One feature on all these machines which would still be easily recognisable from our 1950 visit would be the three point linkage and hydraulic lift, though today this can even be applied to the front of the tractor as well as the rear.

This book tells the story behind the man who made it all happen, Harry Ferguson. It was his ingenuity and inventiveness which took away the old concept of horse drawn implements as applied to tractors and developed the tractor and implement in such a way as they became one unit. There were many benefits once the system had been perfected, and the impact which the

Ferguson System had on agriculture world-wide in the second half of the twentieth century cannot be underestimated.

The journey we take in telling the story is a stormy one, with personalities, politics, economics and even litigation all playing their part. But the main players in the game are the tractors, expressly the 'wee grey Fergie', still held in great affection today as exemplified by the large number of these machines which are either still at work or in active preservation, restored to pristine condition. This book is dedicated not only to the great man himself, Harry Ferguson, but to all those who helped make his dreams a reality.

ACKNOWLEDGMENTS

Many persons and organisations have assisted me in the writing of this book. Special thanks must first go first and foremost to Massey Ferguson (Agco) for their assistance, particularly for the use of some of the black and white photographs which appear in the book. I am most grateful to the Ulster Folk & Transport Museum for access to their collection of pictures relating to Harry Ferguson's early career in Ulster. Andrew Morland, surely the leading photographer of tractors and allied subjects, could not have been more helpful and has supplied many of the superb colour photographs used in the pages which follow. Some of the rarer and earlier images used in the book are far from the quality of Andrew Morland's pictures, but I beg the forbearance of readers for including these, where the historic value outweighs the visual quality. Others who have assisted in many ways are Selwyn Houghton, Rob Ketley, Bob Moorhouse and Steven Moate. My thanks are also due to the many Ferguson and Massey Ferguson users and owners with whom I have had contact over the years, who have gladly shared their experiences with these fine machines..

Harry Ferguson had a flair for good publicity. Ferguson products were advertised with confidence as can be seen from this 1950s example.

This farmer is in trouble

This farmer has a Ferguson

STOP WORRYING about breakdowns — start farming with Ferguson! Ferguson tractors and implements are made of the finest materials. Made to go on *and on* working. And they are backed by Ferguson Service. That means regular inspection and maintenance by *experts*, ensuring that Ferguson equipment is *always* in peak condition.

Find out for yourself what Ferguson can do! Ask your Ferguson Dealer for a free demonstration on your own farm.

QUALITY PAYS—FARM WITH FERGUSON

Chapter One

HARRY FERGUSON – ULSTERMAN EXTRAORDINARY

Harry Ferguson joined his eldest brother Joe's motor business as an apprentice in 1902. In this picture of the firm's staff outside their premises in Little Donegall Street in Belfast, taken around 1905, Harry is astride the motorcycle.

Harry Ferguson built an aircraft in the winter of 1909. He first flew at Hillsborough in County Down on 31st December, managing about 160 yards.

Harry Ferguson was born at Growell, County Down on the 4th November 1884. He was a son of the farm and one of eleven children. He joined his elder brother Joe in his car and motorcycle business in Belfast in 1902 after having considered emigration to the New World. He didn't care much for farm work but soon found a natural aptitude for mechanical work.

Harry was an aviation pioneer and had built and flown his own machine by 1909. After building several aircraft, the demands of married life caused him to give up the dangerous pastime for a less hazardous one, that of racing cars and motor cycles. In 1911 he established May Street Motors and sold the 'Waterloo Boy' tractor in Ireland or the 'Overtime' as it was known in Britain.

His preoccupation with tractors was to take up more and more of his time. In attempting to further his cause in bringing the Ferguson System to the world he not only wooed but was wooed by most of the major tractor manufacturers at some time or other.

A key element in the Ferguson story was the involvement of others. David Brown, Ford Motor Co. and the Standard Motor Co. played an important part in the development of the tractors to which the Ferguson System was applied. Ferguson himself had build up a design team. Willie Sands and Archie Greer were key participants in any developments.

Ferguson moved as the need arose, taking property in Yorkshire during the David Brown years at Honley, near Meltham. His English home became Abbotswood, an estate near Stow on the Wold in Gloucestershire. His English headquarters were at Fletchampstead Highway in Coventry not far from the Banner Lane plant of the Standard Motor Co. where his tractors were built. He held the chair of Massey-Harris-Ferguson Ltd after the merger but resigned once it became clear that his LTX prototypes for a bigger tractor would not reach production.

His activities then centred on other interests including the development of four wheel drive vehicles and the design and construction of racing cars. Harry Ferguson Research had been formed in 1950 and this organisation continued after his death in 1960. One ironic note is that HF Research were involved in the development of the BMC mini tractor. What if Morris Motors had taken up the challenge in the beginning?

But what sort of man was this son of Ulster soil? Like all inventors his behaviour at times was somewhat eccentric. He had fixed ideas about many things. For example he insisted that all involved in his business wore single breasted suits, expressly when demonstrating equipment. He also demanded punctuality at all times and if people turned up late for an appointment, he sometimes would refuse to see them. He suffered from bouts of depression when things weren't going well and whilst giving much inspiration to those he partnered in his business activities, most of these relationships failed when the other parties were driven to exasperation.

Despite these failings, the world has to thank Harry Ferguson for something with which nearly every tractor in 2001 is equipped, the three point linkage and draft control.

Ferguson later moved his aeroplane to Newcastle on the County Down coast. This was hardly a wise place to experiment with aviation. The famous mountains of Mourne, seen in the background, were one obvious potential hazard for such activities.

The original Ferguson plough fitted to a Ford Model T with Eros conversion. The plough was raised mechanically and levelled by the lever seen above the plough between the rear wheels.

The original plough modified for use behind a Fordson tractor.

A later development was the use of three point linkage but the depth was still controlled by a slipper on the plough.

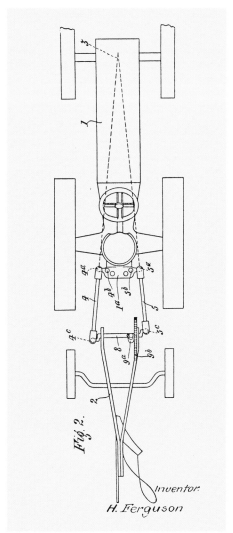

The concept of Ferguson's linkage is show here in a drawing taken from a 1920s patent specification, the numbers on the diagram referring to points in that application. The important thing to note is the transference of weight forward to the front wheels enabled by the fact that the implement is attached to the tractor rather than being drawn by it. This was the fundamental advantage of the Ferguson System which later caused the revolution in the mechanisation of agriculture in large parts of the world in the 1940s and 1950s.

9

Chapter Two

EARLY DAYS

The final design of Ferguson plough attached to a Fordson tractor. Note the lack of any depth wheel or slipper.

A close-up of the plough. Massey Ferguson were still producing a unit of similar appearance in the 1960s.

Towards the end of the Great War, Harry Ferguson found himself working for the Irish Board of Agriculture, involved in a scheme to improve the efficiency of tractor use in Ireland.

He came to the conclusion that the main problem that existed at that time was the complicated design and construction of the ploughs and the tractors, which although extremely crude and heavy, were relatively simple to operate and maintain. When the job was over he decided that he could design a plough far superior to any then in production.

The tractors of which Ferguson had most experience were International Titan and Mogul models, heavy and cumbersome machines, but when Ferguson turned to building his first mechanically operated mounted plough he fitted this to an Eros conversion on the Ford Model T car.

10

This plough was of simple two furrow design mounted on the rear of the tractor, with balance springs so that it could be easily lifted and lowered by the driver using a lever alongside his seat. Unfortunately at the time the plough was launched in late 1917, Ford had started production of his own tractor, later to become the Fordson F, and this killed off any market there might be for this plough.

The original Ferguson plough as preserved by Harry Ferguson's family.

This setback did not deter Ferguson in the least and he set about designing a plough for the Fordson F after he had sold his stock of original ploughs. To overcome the problem of the tractor rearing, which could happen if a trailing plough hit an obstruction, a duplex linkage consisting of two parallel links, was mounted, one above the other, to form a semi rigid arrangement between the tractor and plough. These links were arranged so they pulled the plough down to its working depth and thus enabled the weight of the plough to be kept to a minimum. It improved traction by placing the weight of the plough, and the forces involved in ploughing, firmly on the tractor. One major stumbling block remained, the depth control wheel. These had not been fitted to the Eros and original Fordson ploughs and there was still the problem of keeping the plough at an even depth.

When the plough went into production, made by the Roderick Lean Co. of Mannfield, Ohio, USA, it had to be fitted with a depth wheel. Ferguson was not happy with this and continued, assisted by his development team of Willie Sands, Archie Greer and John Williams, to try and eliminate the depth wheel. Eventually this was achieved by having a floating skid running along the furrow bottom and connected to the duplex linkage so that as the tractor wheels crossed bumps and hollows the movement of the skid caused the plough to be raised or lowered accordingly.

In 1924, shortly after the problem had been solved the Roderick Lean Co. went bankrupt leaving Ferguson without a supplier. This did not deter him and he again set of for America. He had already made various trips there including one to demonstrate his plough to Henry Ford who offered him a job with the Ford Motor Company.

Ferguson now joined forces with the Sherman Brothers, Eber and George, and in 1925 Ferguson Sherman Inc. was formed to produce ploughs in Evansville, Indiana.

Once plough production was running

A Fordson F tractor was also retained by the family to go with the original plough.

smoothly, Ferguson turned his attention to improving his system by adapting it so that various implements, other than ploughs, could be used. The improvements were aimed at removing the balance spring and making the tractor do the work of lifting the implement. Various ideas were tried including an electric motor and a mechanical system driven from the belt pulley through a pair of cone clutches, until finally, a hydraulic system was devised. This was fitted onto the back of a Fordson tractor.

In 1928 Fordson tractor production in the USA ceased and plough production also had to cease. Ferguson was back in Ireland, and did further work on the duplex linkage which was first changed to a three link system with a single lower link and two upper links. The lower link controlled the depth and the two upper links lifted and lowered the implement. The linkage was now fitted to the tractor and not the implement.

Several companies were showing some interest in Ferguson's ideas including Allis Chalmers, Ruston, Ransomes and the Rover Car Co. The most fruitful talks took place with Morris Motors, who agreed to build a tractor using the Ferguson hydraulic system, but at the last minute the agreement fell through. The depression of the late twenties and thirties was having an effect on much of industry at this time.

THE FORDSON TRACTOR

As the Fordson tractor had an important role to play in the development of the Ferguson System, it is worthwhile taking note of the main developments.

Henry Ford always had leanings towards his agricultural roots, but it was not until the age of 44, in 1907, that he assembled his first 'Automobile Plow', using a 1905 Model B car engine, and other B and K car parts. At this stage the Ford Motor Company had no interest, financial or otherwise in the project.

One of Henry Ford's early prototype tractors.

September 1908 saw the introduction of the Model T car, and it was obvious that before long Model T parts would be used to assemble experimental tractors. A number of different designs were assembled using these parts.

It is well known that Henry Ford considered that any tractor ought to have a frame to support the engine and transmission. However, in 1914, one Eugene Farkas, who had been working in Ford's experimental department on the electric car project, was transferred to tractor design work.

Farkas was a pattern maker by trade, and first discussed the possibility of a frameless tractor with Henry Ford in 1915. Charles Sorensen was also involved and he helped Farkas to win Henry Ford over to this concept.

Thus the tractor began to take shape. A new larger engine made by Hercules, was supplied for the first experimental tractors, although there had been at least a design prepared using the Model T engine. The transmission on the Model T prototypes had used a double reduction rear axle. By using a worm drive the necessity for this double reduction axle was removed. Strange that at this stage it disappeared, only to reappear in the English built E27N in 1945, although with the E27N the needs of agriculture had dictated a tractor to do a somewhat different job than those of the 1915 - 17 period.

The first prototype used a three unit construction with engine, gearbox and rear axle joined together by flanges. The worm wheel was also at the top, requiring special lubrication arrangements if the rear axle was not to overheat.

During the process of development, it was suggested that the two halves of the rear axle could be combined. By altering the patterns the gearbox and rear axle casings were made one.

There were probably six prototypes built to the foregoing style, each with small improvements. It is now that we have to move to look at events on the world stage to understand how the final tractors got into production.

The war in Europe had produced an urgent need for alternative means of cultivating the land in Great Britain. Percival Perry, head of Ford in the United Kingdom, had approached Henry Ford to see if production of the new tractor could be started in England, sponsored by the government. Two of the early prototypes had been tried in England with success. These are in fact the Ministry of Munitions models to which name the later batch of 6000 have been wrongly attributed.

Charles Sorensen had actually been dispatched to England in May 1917 to set up production. However, the German Zeppelin raids on London caused government contracts for tractor parts to be cancelled in favour of building fighter planes.

An approach was made to Henry Ford to build the tractors in the USA. There was one snag, the design as it stood had certain weaknesses. These were put right in a further series of prototypes often called the X series.

The cooling system was inadequate so a much bigger radiator, with a cast iron top tank incorporated, was fitted. To simplify things the water pump was dispensed with. The Model T form of low tension ignition was adopted as being more cost effective.

The rear axle tended to overheat, and so the whole ensemble was turned top to bottom, putting the worm in the oil. Underslung worms however tend to aid front end rearing. This was in part overcome by the need to fit a heavier front axle and of course the heavier radiator. To increase ground clearance larger wheels were fitted, 42in instead of previously planned 36in.

Henry Ford had not really wanted to go into production until the tractor had been fully tried out. However his views were overtaken by events. The first tractors were a success, and as production outstripped the means of shipping them to England in the convoys, it was natural that other markets were sought.

The first tractors sold in the USA and Canada were indeed the self same ones as were being shipped to England without any name on, or with 'Henry Ford & Son', stencilled on the radiator.

The name Fordson then appeared, from around April 1919. By the time production had built up and the tractors were being sold domestically, certain changes became apparent on details connected with various components. The first tractors were already at work in England by the time the name Fordson had come into use, and this is what they were all called in retrospect.

It is well known that the early tractors had components supplied by many outside firms. Holley supplied manifolds, Hercules the engines, Cleveland the worm drive and gearbox components came from Timken.

Now it is a different matter to tool up for 6000 units and then have to produce hundreds of thousands. Indeed nearly three quarters of a million Fordsons were to see the light of day by 1928!

The ready availability of the Fordson at an attractive price provided Harry Ferguson with an ideal machine to which to attach his ploughs. Indeed had it not been for the cessation of production in 1928 things might have worked out very differently for Ferguson.

The reasons for the demise of the Model F are complex. Henry Ford liked to have as much control as possible over the sales and service of his machines and in the USA most tractors were sold through Ford car dealerships. Ford was not keen to supply agricultural dealers direct, or give additional discounts to enable his dealers to re-sell tractors to such dealers and industrial converters. Rather than give in to demands by the Ford Dealers Association he announced that the tractor would be discontinued from the end of 1927, a final few being built in 1928.

Fordson tractors being driven by Lord Northcliffe and Henry Ford prior to the agreement to produce tractors in 1917 for Great Britain to help in the war effort.

An early Fordson tractor dating from 1917.

Chapter Three

YORKSHIRE INTERLUDE

The original Ferguson black tractor, seen here after restoration at Fletchampstead, before being placed in the Science Museum in London.

The Ferguson-Brown Type A being demonstrated in Kent.

Ferguson and his associates had been talking of producing a tractor ever since the Fordson ceased production in the USA in 1928. Percival Perry, head of Ford in the United Kingdom, would not supply Fordsons direct from Cork or Dagenham to Ferguson as he felt that it was not in the interests of the Ford Motor Co. to do so.

The result was that Ferguson set about building his own tractor, which was assembled at his May Street, Belfast premises in 1933. Many components were bought in and castings in light alloy from Short's foundry were used. A Hercules engine, David Brown gearbox and Ferguson three point linkage, resulted in a 16 cwt machine as opposed to the 30 cwt of the Fordson.

The Ferguson draft control which was applied to the tractor gave added adhesion when using the Ferguson implements designed specifically for the tractor. It was claimed that there need be no problem as regards the weight of the tractor, except of course, when you towed anything behind. Unit construction was applied and the prototype had this split into four components. The engine, clutch housing, gearbox and rear axle were flanged to each other. The clutch was a single plate unit, and a three speed constant mesh gearbox took the drive to a spiral bevel rear axle, which in design was similar to a lorry rear axle, but with the front cover flange being mated to the rear of the gearbox housing.

Independent brakes were fitted to assist turning and the tractor was mounted on spoked wheels similar to those on the early Fordsons. It could be operated on petrol or kerosene, but the manifold design did not allow for very efficient vapourisation of fuel oils. Ferguson preferred petrol as a tractor fuel anyway!

With a prototype, looking very much like a reduced Fordson, in existence, Ferguson then set about getting the tractor into production. David Brown of Huddersfield had supplied some components for the Black tractor, Ferguson's first prototype machine. Following negotiations, agreement was reached whereby David Brown Tractors Ltd, a new company, would build the tractors and Ferguson would take care of the selling.

The first type production models of the A type tractors, were ready by May 1936. They followed closely the design of the Black tractor. The clutch and gearbox housing were now combined and a Coventry Climax L head engine of 3.125in bore and 4in stroke was now used. This side valve unit ran at 2000rpm and gave 20hp. It featured pressure lubrication and shell bearings. These details gave it a distinct advantage

A Ferguson Type A ploughing with the standard two furrow 12in plough.

A later Type A fitted with pneumatic tyres. The resemblance to the Fordson is remarkable.

over the Fordson engine. Unlike some units built by Climax themselves, a self starter and water pump were absent, on cost grounds, magneto ignition by BTH was used.

The colour of the tractor was changed to battleship grey. Ferguson wanted production models to be black but his staff persuaded him to change.

The location of the hydraulic pump however did create one nuisance in that the hydraulics would only operate when the tractor was on the move and in gear. One had to be on the move when raising the implement and this could be very awkward at headlands when ploughing.

After the first 500 tractors the Coventry Climax concern was retooling for a new engine, so David Brown bought the patterns and built the final 800 or so engines themselves. Four implements were available initially, a 10in two furrow plough, a ridger, and spring or rigid tine cultivators. A single furrow 12in plough came later.

Allied to its own equipment the tractor performed slowly by modern standards but did the job. The engine lacked the guts needed for even two furrow ploughing on heavy land. Its main shortcomings could be allied to bad manifold design which was

later corrected, but not by David Brown, as several proprietary makes of vapourisers were put on the market. Another weakness was the use of alloy castings. Some steel transmission housings were actually cast and some even fitted. This increased the weight of the tractor by about 3cwt. At least one tractor had a PTO fitted, a feature which production tractors lacked.

In the two year period of production David Brown Tractors learnt a lot about the shortcomings of the original design and tried to persuade Harry Ferguson to allow them to build a more powerful tractor. This Ferguson resisted. The two concerns parted company and David Brown started building their own VAK1 model in 1939. Although three point linkage was available on the David Brown tractor, it lacked the draft control of the Ferguson which was protected by patents.

PRODUCTION DATA

Ferguson Black Prototype Tractor
1 only produced 1933.

Ferguson Model A made by David Brown Tractors
1250 made between 1936 and 1938
1-550 Coventry Climax engine.
551-1350 David Brown engine.
(not all the numbers in the sequence were used)

The Type A in detail.

Top left: The engine and driving position showing the manifold and governor.

Above: The nearside of the engine showing oil filter, BTH magneto, and the inevitable toolbox.

Below: The Coventry Climax engine was a sturdy unit but rather unhappy running on paraffin.

Top right: The three point linkage.

Above: The dash showing the throttle lever and serial number plate with Ferguson patents listed.

Below: The radiator, top tank.

Although of similar appearance to the Fordson, the Type A was lower and longer.

The new Type A was also available on pneumatic tyres.

Bottom right: Following the break with Ferguson, David Brown launched their own tractor, the VAK1, in 1939.

Bottom left: A Ferguson Type A preserved in Ulster.

HENRY FORD AND THE FORD MOTOR COMPANY

Henry Ford has an important part to play in the Ferguson tractor story so it is appropriate to include these biographical details.

Born at Greenfield, Michigan on 30th July 1863, he began to work as boy in an engineering shop at Detroit. His first car was a 1896 quadricycle. He rose to be chief engineer at the Edison Illumination Co. and in 1903 founded a business of his own in Detroit. Ford's first two attempts at floating companies failed, but the incorporation of the Ford Motor Company on 16th June 1903, saw the birth of an organisation which would grow into a world leader. Under his presidency, it became the largest maker of automobiles in the world, turning out 3,000 a day and employing 50,000 hands.

The first milestone on the road to success was the launch of the Model T in 1908. It was indeed a conversion of this very car on which Harry Ferguson began his work on mounted ploughs. The Model T lasted in production until 1927. In 1914 Ford instituted a scheme of profit-sharing for his employees, and as regards wages and hours of labour his firm was always most liberal.

In 1915 Ford brought a party of Americans to Europe in the hope of ending the Great War. But later he was convinced of the futility of this policy, and when his country became a belligerent he placed his resources at its disposal, produced war material on a vast scale and subscribed $1,000,000 to the USA Liberty Loan. Meanwhile in 1917 the Fordson tractor, whose history is described elsewhere, went into production.

In December 1918, Henry Ford announced his intention of retiring in favour of his son, one of his new interests being a weekly periodical, *The Dearborn Independent*. Despite this he continued his involvement with the vast company he had created.

His first dealings with Harry Ferguson came in 1920 when a demonstration of the Ferguson plough at Dearborn brought the two men together. Ford, whilst impressed with the plough, looked on Ferguson as a mere tractor salesman and even got Sorenson to offer him a job. What Ferguson really wanted was for Henry Ford to make his plough for him but as Ferguson had refused the offer of employment he was advised to seek other facilities for the manufacture of the plough, which he did.

The retooling for the Model A in 1927 lost Ford a lot of business but expansion was under way elsewhere in the world including the building of Ford's English plant at Dagenham. The Ford V8 was introduced in 1932 and in 1939 the Mercury V8 model was launched. It was this car which provided many of the components, along with others from Ford's truck range, to enable the Ford Ferguson 9N to go into production so quickly.

This tractor, which first entered production in June 1939, was the outcome of the 'Handshake Agreement' between Henry Ford and Harry Ferguson. The 9N was a Ford tractor built in the USA using the Ferguson System. The loss of tractor production in the USA in 1928 had always rankled Ford, who was 76 by the time the 9N started to roll off the production line. He was still active enough to keep full control of the vast organisation as the world was again plunged into war in 1939. Sadly his son Edsel died on 26th May 1943 and grandson Henry Ford II was released from the US navy to return to the Rouge plant in August 1943.

On 23rd January 1944 Henry Ford II was elected executive vice-president of the Ford Motor Company and became its president on 21st September 1945 by which time Henry finally stepped back and retired to Fair Lane, his country residence. After suffering a stroke he died on 7th April 1947.

DEARBORN DAYS

Top right: The prototype Ford Ferguson 9N had rather austere styling.

Below: Henry Ford and Harry Ferguson in discussion at Ford's Fair Lane residence. Ferguson took one of his Type A tractors to Fair Lane to give a demonstration. A model of the tractor is on the table between the two men.

The demonstration of a Type A tractor and plough by Harry Ferguson at Henry Ford's home, Fair Lane, paved the way for the famous 'Handshake Agreement' between the two.

The agreement provided for Ford to build the tractors and Ferguson to market them through his own selling organisation. With the benefit of the most up to date developments in automotive engineering, the Ford design team, along with Ferguson's men Sands and Greer, created the forerunner of the modern tractor, in the model 9N.

To speed production use of standard components was encouraged, and apart from the Ferguson Hydraulic System, the tractor showed its Ford parentage in the use of an engine which was a half size Mercury V8 and a transmission and other components common with other contemporary Ford products. The rear axle design was based on Ford's light truck range and this was to prove a weakness when extra power was required in post TE-20 days.

Prototypes were to hand in March 1939, and by June production models were available for demonstration. The tractor was very much in line with contemporary Ford styling, and the four cylinder side valve engine of 3.125in bore by 3.75in stroke developed 24hp at a maximum speed of 2200rpm. The engine was machined on the same line as the V8 units, an additional shift being put on to cope with the extra production.

Just how much Ferguson's team influenced the design is subject to question, as Ford design policy very much revolved round the 'team' idea, and Ferguson's men just became part of that team. Certainly the hydraulic linkage was pure Ferguson, but the incorporation of the hydraulic pump into a square transmission housing seems to have originated with Sorensen. The beam type front axle was the brainchild of Sands and Greer. Ferguson himself would have liked to have seen an overhead valve engine fitted to the tractor, but the costs of development and the timescale for planned production ruled this out.

The selling organisation which was set up also included the brothers Sherman, who had sold Ferguson ploughs earlier on, and the new selling corporation was in part financed by a loan of $50,000 from Henry Ford.

The tractor was an instant success and put behind it all the weaknesses of the Type A. There was, however, nothing in the agreement in the USA to allow for production of the Ford 9N in the United Kingdom. Ford of Britain were virtually independent of the parent US concern in 1939. Attempts were made to get 9N production started in the UK, but Percival Perry, head of Ford in Britain, did not want to know about Harry Ferguson. This drew him into direct conflict with Henry Ford.

Ford, who was recovering from the after effects of a stroke, was not in full command of the situation. His attempts to force Dagenham to produce the 9N caused a rift between Perry and himself. In any case the matter was in fact outside Perry's hands as the war in Europe had effectively placed tractor production under government control and there was no way the government would allow a break in production to happen.

An early production 9N showing the ease with which the tractor could be handled by a small boy.

The 9N did reach the United Kingdom, fitted with modified Holley 295 Vapouriser to run on TVO and designated the 9NAN. Ford in the UK handled all spares and service on these units imported under Anglo/US lend-lease arrangements.

Wartime shortages caused a utility model to be produced, on steel wheels and without battery reliant electrics or self starter. The 2NAN was the UK equivalent of this model. Edsel Ford, Henry Ford's oldest son, who had a hand in styling the 9N, died in 1943. This left a gap in the Ford empire filled by Henry Ford II in 1945.

The new chairman had the onerous task of putting the Ford operation back into the shape after the ravages of war, and his attitude to the production of a tractor sold by another organisation was hostile. Henry

Not all 9Ns were equipped with the Ferguson system. The tractors illustrated above were among many supplied to US forces during the war.

Ford II realised that the bad business judgement of his grandfather had created the problem, indeed a simple agreement in writing might well have overcome many of the later unpleasantries, therefore the sales agreement was terminated in 1947. The relationship between Ferguson and Ford had sadly deteriorated, not helped by wartime shortages and the end result was that by 1948 Ford were building their own tractor, the 8N, which was simply an improved 9N, and selling it through their own sales organisation.

The new Ford tractor had a four speed rather than a three speed gearbox and improved hydraulics with means of overriding the Ferguson draft control. By this time of course the TE-20 was being built in England, a tractor of very similar design to the 8N.

The termination of the agreement naturally left a situation where Ferguson tractors were no longer being built in America,

and Harry Ferguson was forced to import such tractors as he could from England. He therefore filed a law suite against the Ford Motor Company on 8th January, 1948, regarding the use of the patents held by him in relation to the hydraulic system on the Ford tractor.

The trial started on 29th March, 1951. The sum of $240,000,000 was claimed as a result of the introduction of the Ford 8N and the consequent loss in business to the Ferguson organisation and the unlicensed use of the Ferguson system, which was patented, on the new Ford tractor. After long and costly proceedings, Ferguson accepted a settlement of $9,250,000. This was only to cover the unauthorised use of the Ferguson hydraulic system, the claim against loss of business was dismissed.

The Ford Motor Company were instructed to stop production of the Dearborn or 8N tractor by 1952, but the Ferguson patents had already been extended and were soon to be out of date. Ford's new 1951 model the NAA had a fully 'live' hydraulic system with engine driven hydraulic pump and its introduction necessitated the updating of the then current TO-20 model in due course. Most modern tractors now have the draft control pioneered by Harry Ferguson, usually with the Ford innovation of the overriding feature which allows the lift to be used under 'position control'. This latter feature was not approved by Ferguson, yet from the 35 on, introduced in 1958, it became standard on all Massey-Ferguson models. In due course manufacturers such as Ford and M-F often came to reciprocal agreements over the use of each other's patents. So complex had the situation become over these that M-F and other makers set up their own patents departments run by lawyers to ensure that any new ideas they had were covered, and also to make sure that in building anything new they were not in infringement of anybody else's patented designs.

PRODUCTION DATA

Ford 9N/9NAN/2N/2NAN with Ferguson System

Built Dearborn

1939 (July) 1	1943 107755
1940 14644	1944 131783
1941 47843	1945 174638
1942 92363	1946 204129
	1947 267289
	end 306221

Top right: Later production 9N tractors with the post 1942 style of vertical grille.

Centre right: Ford 2Ns ready for military service in 1943. Such machines were supplied direct to the US forces. This arrangement bypassed Ferguson's sales organisation, something which did not help the already strained relationship between Ford and Ferguson.

Above: The three point linkage on the 9N.

Right: This rear view clearly shows the linkage. Note the rear lamp.

Top left: The badging designed to keep both parties to the 'handshake agreement' happy.

Top right: The 9N engine was in effect half a Mercury V8. Harry Ferguson would have preferred an overhead valve unit.

Above: A right side view of the 9N.

Left: A preserved 9NAN complete with lighting set.

Top: A left side view of a 9N fitted with lighting . Access to the fuel tank was by a service flap.

Above: The steering on the 9N was a unique Ferguson feature which allowed the front track to be adjusted simply.

Left: 9N tractors also featured a central PTO as seen here.

The Ford 8N was virtually the same tractor as the Ford Ferguson.

Improvements to the 8N included a four speed gearbox and the addition of 'position control' to the hydraulic system.

Right: A preserved Ford 8N. The only country in Europe into which 8Ns were imported, was the Irish Free State. Ford UK supplied the rest of the European market with its own British built tractors.

26

The 8N was finished in a beige and red colour scheme which was to be used by Ford in the USA until the early 1960s.

Fergusons in Ulster. A TE-20 and 9NAN together for comparison.

The lawsuit, Harry Ferguson is seen with his legal advisers prior to the court case against Ford. A handshake agreement, such as that made between Henry Ford and Ferguson, was binding in law. Such a simple and unsophisticated procedure was however inappropriate for the complex industrial relationship it was supposed to define. It was almost inevitable that if anything went wrong, matters would finish up in the courts.

Chapter Five

SENT TO COVENTRY

The original Fergie TE-20 with a Continental engine. The steel rear wheels were an accessory. English assembled tractors with Continental engines are easily recognised by the kink in the exhaust pipe.

Following the failure to get 9N production started in the UK, and the breakdown of the 'Handshake Agreement' in the USA, Harry Ferguson was left without a tractor to sell in the United Kingdom. It was fortunate that a surplus capacity in the automotive industry was evident by 1945. Having ceased military work many of the motor manufacturers were looking for ways to use the 'shadow factories' (see page 32) of the war years. Such a plant existed at Banner Lane in Coventry and, approached by Harry Ferguson, Sir John Black, of the Standard Motor Company was receptive to the idea of building tractors there. It was hoped that the whole range of Ferguson implements could also be produced, but with continued government restrictions, there were problems in obtaining the correct tooling and materials.

The TEA-20. Once the Standard engines began flowing from the Canley plant the need for imported units declined.

At the time Standard were about to develop an engine for the new postwar family saloon car, which became the Vanguard, on its appearance in July 1947. This could be adapted to fit a tractor, but in order to get production started engines had to be obtained from elsewhere.

In the postwar years, Britain needed to earn dollars to pay off its wartime debts. The economy was tightly controlled by the government. As the new tractor would primarily be for eastern hemisphere sale this created difficulties with the Ministry of Supply. Licenses and permits had to be obtained to import anything or to purchase any materials, from a washer to a complete machine tool.

An approach to Sir Stafford Cripps, Chancellor of the Exchequer in Britain's new Labour government, was made by Harry Ferguson. Cripps was keen to bring work to Coventry, a city devastated in the blitz. He arranged sanctions for machine tools and raw materials. There was a twist to this however, as the permit for engine imports was only to last until as long as it took to get the new engine into production at Coventry.

Some clever bargaining by Sir John Black with government departments ensured that the engine was sanctioned and it was phased into tractor production in 1948. As the new car was a potential dollar earner, and 60% of production was to be for export, the first engines actually went into the cars, their export in effect countering the import of the American Continental Z-120 engines used on the first production tractors. Early advertising for the Vanguard car even played on the fact that alternative engines were being economically produced for both cars and tractors.

The tractor itself, it was simply an updated 9N with four speed gearbox and an overhead valve engine. Ferguson had managed to obtain a full set of drawings for the 9N during early production and it was on these that the new tractor was based.

THE STANDARD MOTOR CO LTD AND SIR JOHN BLACK

The history of the company dated back to 1903 when it produced its first motor cars at a site on Much Park Street, Coventry. By 1930 the move to Canley had been effected and a range of models were in production, but, like so many others in the motor industry at the time, the depression was having its effects and losses were high.

The man who turned round the company's fortunes was Sir John Black who was appointed its managing director in 1934.

The war affected private car production to such an extent that little work could be done to improve existing models and come the peace in 1945, Standard was still lumbered with its pre-war designs The decision to concentrate on one model for postwar production was a bold one, and the right product had to be found from the outset.

As always in the motor industry cost cutting and savings were important, indeed even in the 1940s development costs of new engines, transmissions and complete vehicles involved high investment in proportion to the expected returns. The 1950s and 1960s boom years in the car industry were to make this problem even worse with the motorist demanding new and innovative models which in turn meant that existing ones had to be updated in some way every year.

Such practices were not possible in the austere economic conditions of the postwar years and Standard concentrated on producing one new model, the Vanguard, which as we shall see, had an immediate effect in bringing the TE-20 tractor into being.

Harry Ferguson and Sir John Black pose for the press in front of the Ferguson System on the TE-20.

The classic TEA-20, fitted with a Standard engine, complete with transport box. Although the general styling followed that of the Ford-Ferguson, the Coventry built product always looked neater.

A nearside view of the same tractor. The toolbox was an important feature, most of the nuts on tractor and implements could be tightened with one wrench.

The two furrow plough attached to a TED-20 petrol/TVO model. The vertical exhaust on this tractor is a later feature.

While Harry Ferguson was preoccupied with his legal battles in the western hemisphere, production at Banner Lane built up satisfactorily, and in due course all the tractors built were equipped with Standard engines. In the context of the agricultural industry the terms western and eastern hemispheres were used to define particular sales areas. The western hemisphere included the USA, Canada, South and Central America. Indeed the new plant was, at the time, the most modern vehicle production facility in Europe with the ability to turn out 300 units a day or around 100 a shift. Components were drawn from a wide range of suppliers and the fully automated production line was able to draw these from the stores in a highly organised manner to keep production line flowing. Many

components were primed and paint dipped before assembly and the finished tractor carcasses were sprayed and then baked before going on to final assembly when tinwork and wheels were added.

It was then over to the sales team to go to work. Ferguson's flair for publicity rubbed off in all areas from newspaper advertising to a series of films promoting the new tractor and its implements. As to the competition ask any Ford salesman of the late forties and early fifties what he feared most and he would tell you, 'The Grey Menace'. Such was the success of the product of this new relationship between Harry Ferguson and the Standard Motor Company, it provided the Irishman with a tractor which, for the first time, challenged the supremacy of Ford in the United Kingdom. The only

BANNER LANE

The rise of Adolf hitler and the Nazi Party in Germany in the 1930s saw the British government take steps towards rearmament. Part of this rearmament programme involved the creation of a number of so called 'shadow factories' up and down the country. The idea behind these facilities was that they could be turned to wartime munitions production if the need arose. They were often located away from industrial centres to make them less susceptible to wartime air attack. Such a plant was built by the government at Banner Lane, to the north west of Coventry, in 1938. The 80 acre site had covered buildings with internal space of 1.2 million square feet. It was used for aero engine production during the war. The factory was prepared for production of the Ferguson tractor at a cost in excess of £3 million.

The Banner Lane production line at Coventry with TE-20 assembly in full swing. The line could turn out over 300 tractors a day.

problem was that the tractor ran on petrol and the sales boys peddling the competition made good use of this. Petrol was still rationed in 1946, indeed it was 1950 before all restrictions on its use were lifted. Enough fuel could be obtained in the usual way for agricultural use, but it was subject to excise duty, whereas Tractor Vapourising Oil, was not.

Harry Ferguson was initially against a low cost fuel variant, but as the home market gradually opened up it became necessary to add the TED-20 to the range. Rebated petrol had been available for agricultural use during the war but was withdrawn in 1949. The alternative was TVO, but this required an engine with a lower compression ratio and suitable vapouriser. Indeed once the TVO model had been established, a zero octane (lamp oil) model was also offered for export from 1950.

The petrol engine developed 28.4hp at the belt and was of 3in bore and 3½ stroke. Now the car version of the engine was, after initial development, set at 85mm. Again Ferguson was not keen to increase the power output of the tractor. He was want to point out that it defeated the object of the exercise.

A prize winning restoration of a Fergie 20. The self starter and coil ignition were revolutionary features on tractors for the UK market when the Fergie was first launched in 1946.

The TVO model was only rated at 26hp at the belt, and it was pointed out that by using the larger bore engine, the power could be increased to that of the petrol version. This was agreed, but when the change to the 85mm engine took place on 22nd January 1951, at serial number 172501, the larger engine was fitted to all spark ignition models.

With the competition fitting diesels in production models, it was not long before Ferguson's sales force were calling for a diesel version of the TE-20. Now as Harry Ferguson himself was not a diesel fan, it took some considerable persuasion to get him to agree to a diesel engined tractor at all.

Although the source of the petrol and TVO engines for the TE-20 tractors built at Banner Lane was of course the same, the Standard Motor Company, Ferguson was under no obligation to buy engines from that concern. At the time the only really suitable engine available was the Perkins P3, and this was still under development. Perkins offered the P4, but it was a rather expensive item, (as was the P3), and developed too much power in the eyes of Harry Ferguson. Freeman Sanders became involved in the design work on the diesel engine which was commissioned initially by Ferguson. Part of the deal was that development costs would be shared equally if the same engine could be adapted for use in the Vanguard car. In the end Ferguson had to bear all the development costs, as by the time the car went diesel, Massey Harris had become involved on the tractor side.

The resultant unit was dry linered and had a bore and stroke of $3\frac{5}{16}$in x 4in. It had an indirect injection layout, chain driven camshaft and fuel injection pump, and turned out some 2cwt heavier and 1.25in longer than the petrol version. This meant that it was not possible to provide units to convert previous production tractors to diesel, as the building of the TEF-20, as it

A restored TED-20. There is much controversy regarding the correct shade of grey for restoration purposes.

Two publicity shots of the TED-20, taken in the experimental shop at Fletchampstead showing clearly the tin shield over the vapouriser.

was designated on its introduction in June 1951, had to take these dimensional variations into account. Kigass equipment was provided to aid starting, but even with this feature the engine had a reputation for sluggish starting in cold weather. A single heater plug was situated in the inlet manifold. Strange to say, when the engine was finally fitted in the Vanguard car in 1955, separate heater plugs for each cylinder were provided. Some engines of this type did eventual-

ly get into a few tractors. The only effect that this had on other models was the adaptation in 1952, for all variants, of 12 volt electrics, from serial number 250001 onwards. This was in any case only following the trend in general for 12 volt systems in the whole motor industry.

In addition to the standard tractor, demand grew for narrower versions once its potential for use in vineyards and orchards was realised. The factory built narrow version came out in 1946. This lost 6in in width by the fitting of narrower axle shafts. In 1952 the vineyard model became a factory assembled option and by the use of smaller tyres, a reduction in overall height of 2in was achieved in addition to a reduced width of 32in minimum track.

The diesel model was never offered in

Industrial models were built too. This is a semi-industrial model TEP-T20 fitted with a 'banana' loader equipped with a gravel bucket.

The full industrial model complete with all round fenders is seen here and featured dual brakes (hydro mechanical), bumper, grille guard and industrial tyres.

narrow or vineyard form in TE-20 days, although conversions were offered by Reekie Engineering, Jack Oldings and others. These firms had started by converting standard spark ignition tractors, indeed some Ford/Ferguson 9Ns were also dealt with.

By the early fifties tractors were also becoming more common in industry and a whole range of allied equipment was advertised for use with the Ferguson, from mobile compressors to a complete drive on roller. A plethora of variations were offered for industrial

A close-up of the Standard diesel engine showing the fuel system. It was not possible to convert existing tractors to diesel with this engine.

Opposite page:

Top: A restored example of the TEF-20 diesel. The standard diesel engine was some 1.25in longer and 2cwt heavier than the petrol version

Bottom: A semi industrial TET-T20 in the livery of Surrey County Council.

THE FERGUSON HYDRAULIC LIFT

When the control lever is pushed forwards, the cam portion bears on the top of the control fork, which pivots at A, thus the control valve is pulled to the rear or drop position. When the tool enters the ground the top link is pushed against the control spring. Forward movement of the implement compresses the control spring and moves the pivot point A forwards and thus moves the control valve to a given depth of working determined by the distance forward of the control lever. The compression on the control spring is just sufficient to return the control valve to neutral, in which position the weight of the implement is held on the tractor and the implement cannot go any deeper. If the front wheels enter a depression, the control spring expands, thus allowing the control valve to come slightly out of the pump and the implement to lower sufficiently to maintain its depth. On the other hand, if the front wheels rise onto higher ground, the control spring is further compressed and the control valve lifts the implement slightly in relation to the front wheels.

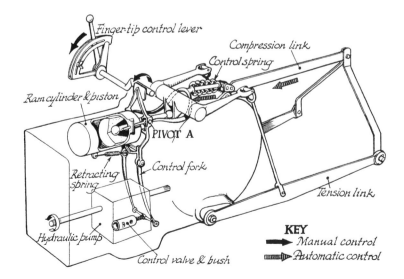

Finger-tip control lever

Compression link

Control spring

Ram cylinder & piston

PIVOT A

Retracting spring

Control fork

Tension link

Hydraulic pump

Control valve & bush

KEY
→ Manual control
⟶ Automatic control

FLETCHAMPSTEAD HIGHWAY

Although the Ferguson tractor was built at Banner Lane, another 'shadow' site became the headquarters of Harry Ferguson Ltd. Originally known as the Fletchampstead North Works, these premises were situated just off Tile Hill Road in Coventry and had been used for

An ariel view of 'Fletch' as it was affectionately known by Standard employees.

aircraft production during the war; those employees with a penchant for golf having to give up the works course in the process as the factory was built on the site.

Whilst the whole of the Ferguson design, sales and administration teams were housed in the office block, the rest of the premises provided space for workshops used by the experimental and test departments. Ferguson also employed his own photographic staff, many photographs of machinery from the 1940s and 1950s include the factory's railings in the background. Many of the other photographs of tractors and implements were taken within the works with sheets suitably arranged to 'white out' the background.

paid to the US market as far as Ferguson was concerned. The production capacity of Ford, now that they had ceased to supply Ferguson, and launched the new 8N Dearborn tractor complete with its range of implements, would build some 442,000 plus units from between 1947 and 1952. This tractor was based on the 9N but had an extra speed and improved hydraulics.

In the meantime, Ferguson had acquired a small plant near Detroit, and in October 1948 production of the TO-20 (the TO stood for, tractor overseas) was started. This was very similar to the TE-20 and used the same Continental Z-120 engine. Naturally sub-assemblies and electrical components came from US suppliers. A number of TE-20 tractors were imported from Britain in 1947. This is one of the reasons why, despite the Standard engine being used in UK production from 1947, some tractors equipped with the Continental Z-120 engine continued to be built at Coventry until July 1948. In the United States some 60,000 TO-20 tractors were built up to August 1951. In the same period Ford built and sold seven times that number of 8N tractors!

use, from basic tractors to those with full front and rear fenders and extra braking and lighting to comply with the Road Traffic Acts.

Everybody thought that the TE-20 would go on for ever, but already, as we have seen, the model had been effectively superseded in the western hemisphere. Over half a million Grey Fergies were built from 1946 to 1956, at the time the largest production run of any tractor in the United Kingdom.

The end of the relationship between Henry Ford and Harry Ferguson almost put

38

A publicity shot of a production TEF-20 showing the additional air cleaner fitted to the diesel tractor.

The TET-T20 industrial model. Note the battery location, standard on all diesel models.

Ferguson tractors worked worldwide tackling hundreds of jobs. Here we see climatic contrasts with a TEF-20 discing in the West Indies, and nearer home, a TEF-20 fitted with wheel girdles and a front blade.

FERGUSON

does the impossible

IN THE
ANTARCTIC

The 1954 Antarctic expedition made use of Ferguson tractors and this publicity brochure was produced to commemorate the achievements.

Copy of a report by John Russell, Engineer, Mawson Station, during 1954, and endorsed by Mr. P. G. Law, Director of Antarctic Division

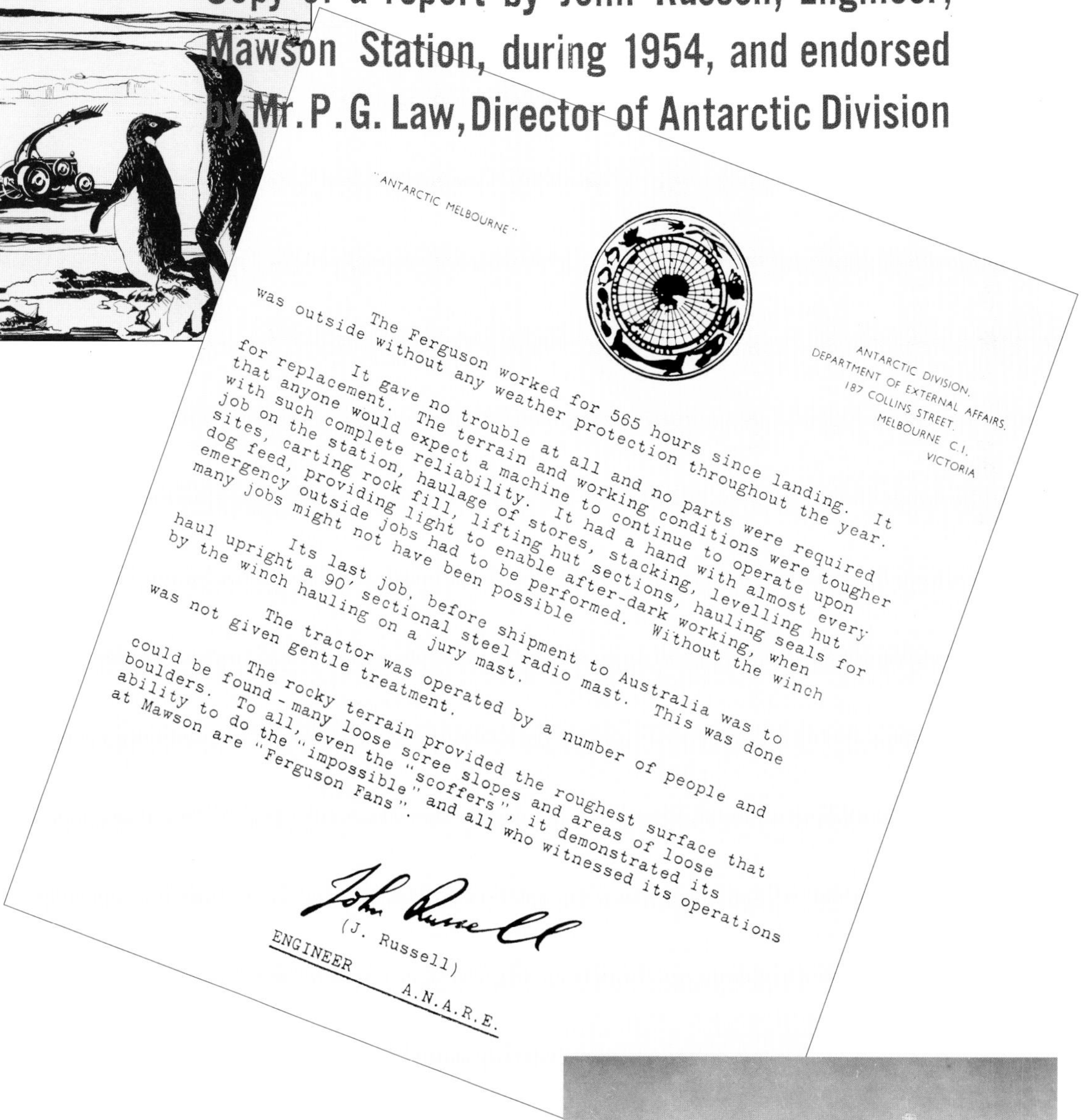

"ANTARCTIC MELBOURNE"

ANTARCTIC DIVISION,
DEPARTMENT OF EXTERNAL AFFAIRS,
187 COLLINS STREET,
MELBOURNE C.I.
VICTORIA

The Ferguson worked for 565 hours since landing. It was outside without any weather protection throughout the year.

It gave no trouble at all and no parts were required for replacement. The terrain and working conditions were tougher that anyone would expect a machine to continue to operate upon with such complete reliability. It had a hand with almost every job on the station, haulage of stores, stacking, hauling seals for dog feed, carting rock fill, lifting hut sections, levelling hut sites, providing light to enable after-dark working, when emergency outside jobs had to be performed. Without the winch many jobs might not have been possible.

Its last job, before shipment to Australia was to haul upright a 90' sectional steel radio mast. This was done by the winch hauling on a jury mast.

The tractor was operated by a number of people and was not given gentle treatment.

The rocky terrain provided the roughest surface that could be found - many loose scree slopes and areas of loose boulders. To all, even the "scoffers", it demonstrated its ability to do the "impossible", and all who witnessed its operations at Mawson are "Ferguson Fans".

(J. Russell)
ENGINEER   A.N.A.R.E.

Unloading stores from the supply ship.

40

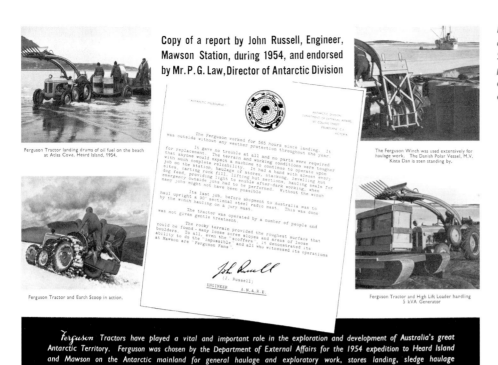

Copy of a report by John Russell, Engineer, Mawson Station, during 1954, and endorsed by Mr. P. G. Law, Director of Antarctic Division

Ferguson tractors later made a 1200 mile journey to the South Pole in 1957-58. This page shows the earlier activities of the Australian expedition to Heard Island.

Ferguson Tractor landing drums of oil fuel on the beach at Atlas Cove, Heard Island, 1954.

The Ferguson Winch was used extensively for haulage work. The Danish Polar Vessel, M.V. Kista Dan is seen standing by.

Ferguson Tractor and Earth Scoop in action.

Ferguson Tractor and High Lift Loader handling 5 kVA Generator

Ferguson Tractors have played a vital and important role in the exploration and development of Australia's great Antarctic Territory. Ferguson was chosen by the Department of External Affairs for the 1954 expedition to Heard Island and Mawson on the Antarctic mainland for general haulage and exploratory work, stores landing, sledge haulage and survey work — another great tribute to Ferguson Versatility and Reliability.

OFFICIAL FERGUSON TRACTOR REPORT

Tractor off-loaded from Kista Dan onto sea-ice at Mawson, MacRobertson Land, 13th February, 1954. Temperature 10° below zero . . . Tractor started instantly and hauled load to shore over sea-ice and tide-crack . . . Tractor is in constant use—hauling sledges, lifting and stacking cases . . . Winch used to handle heavier loads over rocks . . . Heaviest haul for Winch was Diesel Generators which weighed approximately $2\frac{3}{4}$ tons . . . High Lift Loader in constant use, lifting and carrying, also ' Bulldozing ' blasted rock to clear building sites. The Ferguson hauled and lifted into position large sections of the prefabricated huts ; also acted as a portable scaffold for men fixing roof sections. Several occasions tractor completely covered with drift—but

after clearing snow away from the controls tractor started instantly (even though engine was snowed over). Tractor parked on hillside in full blast of wind and drift . . . Tractor used on plateau ice slopes which rise in sweeps of 1 in 9 and 1 in 7 at the steepest grades—in 3 miles one rises to 1,800 feet. These slopes are hard polished ice—a man cannot walk on same without crampons . . . Air temperature 42° below zero. Ice slopes climbed in 1st and 2nd gears without overloading motor.

On December 7th, Ferguson hauled a spare track for a Weasel which was stranded 50 miles south—up the ice slopes to Mt. Henderson. The dogs could not haul up the ice slopes and the Ferguson saved the day.

Tractor shipped for return to Australia, 25th February, 1955.

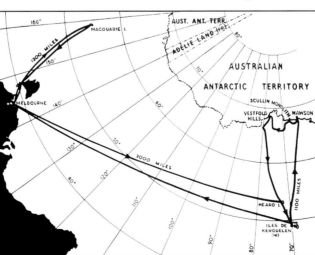

CONTINENTAL ENGINES

There were delays in getting the Canley plant in Coventry retooled for production of the new Standard engine which was to be fitted in both the Vanguard car and the Ferguson tractor. This meant that initial TE-20 production was powered by Continental engines imported from the United States.

Continental was one of a number of manufacturers in the USA, such as Buda, Hercules, Waukesha and Detroit, who produced engines of all types for the motor industry.

Some products of these concerns were built and designed especially to suit particular applications, but in the case of the Ferguson tractor, an existing 120 cubic inch capacity engine was developed for use in the tractor.

The Continental Motors Corporation had plants at Detroit and Muskegan in Michigan. Their 'Red Seal' range of engines had become well established before the war. These engines had been used by other tractor manufacturers, notably Massey Harris. The relationship between Continental and Ferguson was to continue in the USA until the 1960s as most spark ignition Ferguson and Massey Ferguson tractors built at the Ferguson Detroit plant were powered by Continental engines.

TE-20 Model Designations.

TE-20	Standard built tractor with Continental Z-120 engine, 1946-48
TEA-20	Standard built tractor with Standard petrol engine, 1947-56
TO-20	Detroit built tractor with Continental Z-120 engine, 1948-51
TEB-20	Standard built tractor with Continental engine, narrow, 1946-48
TEC-20	Standard built tractor with Standard engine, narrow, 1948-56
TED-20	Standard built tractor with V. O. Standard engine, 1949-56
TEE-20	Standard built tractor with V. O. Standard engine, narrow, 1949-56
TEF-20	Standard built tractor with Standard diesel engine, 1951-56
TO-30	Detroit built tractor with Continental Z-129 engine, 1951-54
TEH-20	Standard built tractor with Standard Zero Octane engine, 1950-56
TEJ-20	Standard built tractor with Standard Z.O. engine, narrow, 1950-56.
TEK-20	Standard built tractor with Standard petrol engine, vineyard, 1952-56
TEL-20	Standard built tractor with Standard V.O. engine, vineyard, 1952-56
TEM-20	Standard built tractor with Standard Z.O. engine, vineyard, 1952-56
TEP-20	Standard built tractor with Standard petrol engine, industrial, 1952-56
TER-20	Standard built tractor with Standard V.O. engine, industrial, 1952-56
TES-20	Standard built tractor with Standard Z.O. engine, industrial, 1952-56
TET-20	Standard built tractor with Standard diesel engine, industrial, 1952-56

Engines used in TE-20 production.

Make and Model	Cyls	Bore and Stroke	CC	Fuel	HP	Used on.
Cont. Z-120	4	81mm x 95mm	1966	G	23.9	TE-20/TO-20
Standard	4	80mm x 92mm	1850	GG/K	23.9	TEA-20 etc.
Standard	4	85mm x 92mm	2088	GG/K	28.2	TEA-20 etc.
Cont. Z-129	4	3.25in x 3.875in	2113	G	30.27	TO-30
Standard	4	80.96mm x 101.6mm	2092	D	26.00	TEF-20

Notes: G=Gasoline.   G/K= Petrol/TVO.
D=Diesel.   TD=Turbocharged Diesel.

Ferguson TE-20 model
Built by Standard Motor Company

1946	1	1950	116462	1954	367999
1947	315	1951	167837	1955	428093
1948	20895	1952	241336	1956	488579
1949	77773	1953	310780	end	517651

First Standard engine used September 1947.
TE (Continental) and TEA (Standard) engined
tractors were built side by side up to serial
number 48000.
Last Continental engine used, July 1948.
First TED (VO) model built, April 1949.
85mm engine (petrol and TVO) introduced
from serial number 172501, 22nd January 1951.
First TEF (diesel) model built January 1951.
12 volt electrics phased in from serial number
250001

Ferguson TO-20/TO-30
Built by Harry Ferguson Inc. Detroit

1948	(Oct) 1	1951	39163	1954	125959
1949	1808	1952	72680	end	140000
1950	14660	1953	108645		

TO-30 began production from serial number
60001 in August 1951.

Prices

Ferguson TE-20	(12/46)	£343.00
Ferguson TEA-20	(10/50)	£335.00
Ferguson TED-20	(10/50)	£335.00
Ferguson TED-20	(10/51)	£370.00
Ferguson TEF-20	(10/51)	£490.00

THE STANDARD VANGUARD

This car, announced in July 1947, was a completely new design which
eventually replaced the entire range of Standard models inherited from the
pre-war period. Its ethos was very much with exports to world markets in mind
and the finished product could have easily been a scaled down model from
one of the US car builders. In original form the rear boot was incorporated into
the stylish lines of the bodywork. The engine was basically the same as that
used in the Ferguson TE-20, but an 85mm bore was adopted following tests
with the prototypes. Naturally, other engine details differed such as the
carburettor, but the fact that the engine was 'wet' linered was an unusual
feature for a private car. Needless to say the engine ran at much higher
speeds with a rating of 68hp at 4200 rpm., but bearing surfaces were more
than adequate for this.

Most Vanguard production went overseas in 1948 and 1949 but from 1950
the car appeared in increasing numbers on Britain's roads. An estate version
had meanwhile been added to the range. The basic saloon sold for £658, a
de-luxe version at £765. Laycock overdrive was also available as an extra.

The phase one version lasted in production until early 1953 when the booted phase two
model was introduced. An important addition to the range in early 1954 was the availability of
the diesel engine in the car; this added 2cwt. to the total weight. This engine was very similar
to that introduced in the TEF-20 tractor in early 1951 but benefited from the provision of a
heater plug for each cylinder. The performance of the diesel version of the car was pedestrian
compared with petrol engined models. The price, at £1099 in the UK, meant that most went
abroad. The phase two model continued in production until late 1955. The phase three
Vanguard, when introduced in October 1955, retained the basic 85mm engine but had a
completely new monocoque bodyshell.

Van and pickup versions of the Vanguard were also available and special terms were
offered to Ferguson dealers who added many of these to their parts and service fleets. A
Ferguson salesman of the early 1950s was thus quite likely to arrive on your farm behind the
wheel of Vanguard.

STANDARD VANGUARD

The Family Car—
popular everywhere

THE STANDARD MOTOR COMPANY LTD., COVENTRY
London: 13, Davies St., Grosvenor Square, W.1. Tel: May. 3011
STANDARD CARS · STANDARD COMMERCIAL VEHICLES · FERGUSON TRACTORS · TRIUMPH CARS
—All that's best in Britain.—

Chapter Six

MERGER WITH MASSEY

The TO-35 introduced in the USA in 1954 retained the tilting bonnet of the TE-20.

Massey Harris had enjoyed mixed fortunes in the postwar tractor market in the USA as this was far more competitive than that in the UK in those years. Masseys postwar models were not popular with the customers and it was felt that the Ferguson System would overcome these difficulties. In fact

The Fergie 20 family assembled, from left to right, TE-20, TO-20, TO-30, TO-35, FE-35 and F-40.

Harry Ferguson had approached Massey Harris back in 1947 with regard to taking over the US production of the T-20 but the offer was declined. The first steps involved M-H taking over Ferguson's Detroit plant but soon these early plans moved forward to a situation where full scale merger talks ensued. A final hurdle had to be overcome however, as Harry Ferguson valued his business at $17million whilst Massey Harris offered $16million.

The score was finally settled whilst passing through Broadway in Worcestershire as Ferguson travelled to a demonstration with M-H's senior management. Ferguson suggested that tossing a coin could bring things to a conclusion and outside the Lygon Arms Hotel a coin was spun. Ferguson lost but won a toss for the coin itself which was later mounted on a silver cigar box and presented to Harry by his friends.

Although the lawsuit with Ford had the effect of causing the production of the 8N to be stopped, Ford were ready for this and launched a new model in late 1952, the NAA. Ferguson was also prepared for this in the USA and launched the TO-30 in August 1951. This used the larger Continental Z-129 engine which had a 3.25in bore and 3.875in stroke. Hydraulics were improved. The Scotch yoke piston type pump worked at up to 2300psi on all US built Ferguson TO-20s and 30s. Continental remained the main source for engines in the Detroit built

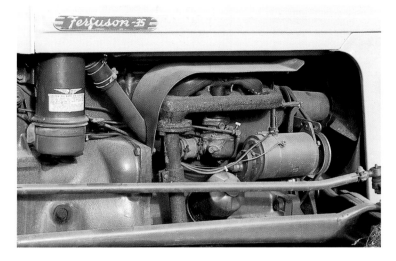

tractors until the diesel and Perkins took over in the late fifties.

In 1954 the TO-35 was introduced. The Z134 Continental engine now had a bore stretched to 3⅜in. Like all US built Ferguson tractors to date it retained six volt electrics, but had a redesigned gearbox with six forward speeds and an improved four piston hydraulic pump. Position control was introduced to the hydraulics. This

The Continental engine fitted to the TO-35. Due to the low cost of gasoline, diesels didn't take a hold on the US market until the early 1960s.

The green and grey colour scheme of the TO-35 was to avoid confusion with the red and grey Ford 8N.

QUADRAMATIC CONTROL

DUAL-RANGE TRANSMISSION

Some of the new features of the 35 are shown in the numbered panels.

It was 1956 before the new model 35 was available in England. This TVO version is kitted out as a semi-industrial.

VARIABLE-DRIVE PTO

TWO-STAGE CLUTCHING

was done as Ford models from 1948 had been thus equipped, and despite this facility effectively 'locking out' the Ferguson draft control, by now Harry Ferguson was only a part of the Massey Harris Ferguson concern, and market demands, in the western hemisphere at least, held sway. The TO-35 retained the TO-20 appearance, but was finished in a green and grey colour scheme in deference to the then Ford colours of red and grey. A diesel version, using imported Standard 23C engines, was also offered. Production at Ferguson's Dearborn plant never reached that of Banner Lane, in fact by the end of the TE-20 in 1956, Coventry had built 517,651 units and Dearborn only 169,000.

It was 1956 before a new model came to the United Kingdom. The TO-35 came onto a market where a 'two line' policy was operated, in the western hemisphere. Massey Harris models continued in production for sale through former Massey dealers. Ferguson machines being sold separately through Ferguson dealers.

It so happened, that after the merger, Massey Harris dealers in the USA, mainly due to the unpopularity of the then current M-H range, asked for a Massey version of the Fergie.

The result was the Massey Harris 50, which was simply a Ferguson TO-35 altered to provide a rowcrop beam style front axle, which could also be replaced by a single front wheel or vee twin wheels, increased ground clearance and provided with Massey Harris style tinwork.

There was a resultant backlash from the Fergie dealers in the USA to this model, leading to the creation in 1956 of the Fer-

The British version of the 35 had a fixed bonnet and revised styling. The grey and gold colour scheme was exclusive to this model.

The 23C diesel engine fitted to the 35 proved to be a bad starter. Access to the bonnet was by a service flap.

guson 40. This was pure Ferguson, without any Massey characteristics. It had distinctive new tinwork and was sold through the Ferguson dealers.

From 1958 the two line policy was phased out and the two models were abandoned in favour of a revised Massey Ferguson 50 finished in red and metallic grey, but with styling more in keeping with the Massey-Harris tradition. In addition the

A Ferguson 35 with a tipping trailer. The trailer had the wheels at the rear to facilitate weight transfer to the rear wheels of the tractor.

Perkins 3 cylinder 3A-152 diesel was fitted to this machine. The Massey Ferguson 65 Dieselmatic introduced at the same time in the USA used the Perkins 4 cylinder 4A-203 engine and had almost identical styling. From 1960 the 65 diesel sold in the USA became identical with its European counterpart, and in due course this received the improved, direct injection Perkins AD4.203 engine. The MF-35 diesel also adopted the Perkins 3A-152 engine.

By fitting the Perkins 4.192 engine to the Massey-Harris 50 carcass, the Massey Ferguson Dieselmatic 65 was introduced in the USA. Frontal styling was halfway between

A 1956 sales brochure for the Ferguson 35 as sold in the USA.

Top: The Ferguson 40 was exclusive to the western hemisphere Ferguson dealerships and provided row crop features with the Ferguson System. This is a standard model.

Above: The tricycle version is seen here. Both tractors illustrated have Continental gasoline engines. The small illustrations, (right) taken from the sales brochure, show alternative front axle arrangements.

Ferguson and M-H tradition. In fact, apart from the improved gearbox there was little more to this machine than the Ford Ferguson 9NAN into which Frank Perkins fitted a P4 for his own use during the war. It took another ten years or so for the power to be applied to basically the same transmission.

To provide the UK with a similar tractor, the press tools for the 40 tinwork were shipped to the Banner Lane plant, and thus the 65 in Britain took on the appearance of the erstwhile Ferguson 40, with important differences.

Double reduction hubs were provided at the end of the axle shafts and disc brakes fitted.

Later 65s received the Perkins AD4.203 engine which was now direct injection and developed 58.38hp at 2000rpm. The original engine put out 50.5hp.

A final feature of late series 35 and 65 tractors was 'Multipower'. This doubled the number of working speeds. A hydraulically operated high/low range with on the move shift capability was fitted ahead of the main transmission train. A separate hydraulic pump, mounted on top of the main tractor hydraulic pump in the rear transmission, provided the power source. One design flaw was that engine braking was not available in low range, a weakness which the author of this book found to his cost on one occasion.

Industrial models of both the 35 and 65 were produced and these had the option of torque convertor transmission. The 35 was also produced in vineyard form, with a diesel engine being available on this model for the first time.

After the merger, in the United Kingdom, where dealer structures were somewhat different, many Massey-Harris dealers found themselves selling Ferguson tractors after 1954. The situation also arose where some dealers sold Fordson tractors and Massey Harris implements. There were not that many Massey-Harris tractors sold in the UK anyway! Changes in the Ford policy regarding dealers, with a move away from their car and truck dealers selling tractors, unknowingly helped some dealers to change to 'grey'.

The late 1956 introduction of the FE-35 brought this new model onto the British market. Its appearance however was rather later than had been anticipated.

A Fergie 35 fitted with a Perkins P3(TA) engine as a development tractor. For the full story of the Perkins involvement with Massey Ferguson see Chapter 7..

The end of the two line policy not only saw all models rebadged as Massey Ferguson but the 35 in the UK received a new red and grey colour scheme as well as a Perkins P3.152 engine from 1958.

US built models also adopted the new colour scheme but the grey finish was metallic.

The MF-35X featured the more powerful Perkins A3.152 engine and was launched in 1962.

Petrol engined MF35s, such as the example seen here, were also produced.

Multi Power was an important option on MF tractors from 1959.

Colour schemes compared. Here are the US built TO-35 and the British built FE-35.

Vineyard models were built in France. This is a MF-35 with 23C diesel engine.

53

Above: For industrial use the red paint dip of bonnet and wings was replaced by yellow. Note the industrial tyres and fenders. British local authorities were the main customers for this model.

Below: TE-20s were also finished in yellow. This is an industrial TEP-20T with a front road sweeping attachment. The brush was mechanically driven from the tractor PTO.

Unlike its US counterpart, the TO-35 the FE-35 featured revised styling, and instead of a tilting bonnet it had a service flap to gain access to the fuel tank(s). The TVO and petrol engines were now of 87mm bore and were rated at 30/34hp. The diesel had the new 23c engine which now had a bore of 84.14mm and was rated at 37hp at 2000rpm. In due course a dual clutch and 'live' PTO were offered as options.

Finished in a grey and gold colour scheme the new model looked very smart, but the diesel version soon gained a reputation for being a bad starter. Harry Ricardo had been brought in to improve the engine and it seemed that the 'improvements' had a detrimental effect!

The Massey Ferguson hierarchy were none too happy that the Banner Lane plant was not in their ownership. Protracted negotiations started in 1957 to take over the plant; this did not involve the engine production facility.

It so happened around that time that F. Perkins Ltd of Peterborough were passing through troublesome times. The onslaught of own make diesel engines, coupled with the success of Ford's new 590E and 592E engines, plus the drying up of the conversion pack market, was taking its toll on the firm. By acquiring Perkins, Massey Ferguson had the opportunity of obtaining the capacity to supply diesel engines for both its eastern and western hemisphere operations. Until that time, US built tractors still used Continental diesel engines.

By 1958/9, both Banner Lane and the Peterborough plant of F Perkins were under MF control. Faced with a drying up of sales for its engines, the Standard Motor Company now considered building its own tractors; indeed prototypes were even built. The implement manufacturer, New Idea, was involved in this scheme. The planned range of implements and the tractor never came to anything. In the end Standard had to be content in selling their 23C

engines to Allis Chalmers for the ED40. They continued to supply petrol engines to MF, and also to Ford for their Dexta.

Perkins had successfully updated their P3 engine for use in the Ford Dexta, and at the same time took the opportunity of revising their own production unit. The result was the P3/144, a development of which very soon found its way into the Ferguson 35 as the P3/152.

Gone were the cold starting problems associated with the 23C engine and the 35

The MF65 was the big tractor launched in 1958 which gave M-F a model to compete directly with the Fordson Major.

settled down to a successful run which lasted until it was superseded by the 135 in 1965. During that time further improvements were made. 'Live' hydraulics and PTO also made their appearance, and in 1962 the 35X, with the more powerful Perkins A3/152 engine, was introduced. Even after Perkins came under M-F control, engines were still supplied to Ford for both the Dexta, Super Dexta and other applications; indeed other tractor manufacturers as well still fitted Perkins engines.

The scene was now set to provide the basis for the next generation of tractors, apart from the fact that the French M-F plant, inherited through Massey Harris, launched their own small tractor in 1963, the 25. This tractor had been developed

Above: The US built 65 sales leaflet shows different styling and in this case a Continental petrol engine fitted.

Right: Power for the MF-65 was provide by the Perkins 4.192 engine. Note the rotary CAV fuel pump.

Below: The MF-65 adopted the tinwork previously used on the Ferguson 40 for Coventry production.

CONVENIENCE

TRACTORMETER

using a four cylinder Perkins 4.99 engine in a Fergie 20, the final model receiving the slightly larger 4.107 engine. This tractor was also known as the 30 and the 825 during its short production run. One unusual feature of this model was the location of the hydraulic pump in the top housing of the transmission.

In addition to normal models, the M-H-F 202 and Massey Ferguson 202 and 204 were offered in the USA. These models were for industrial and commercial use and featured

Far left: The tractormeter on the MF-65 showed how fast the engine, belt and TPO were turning and how many hours the tractor had worked.

A classic scene with the MF-65 and a Massey Ferguson PTO driven baler.

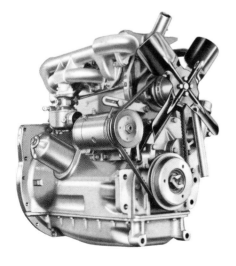

optional power steering. The 204 had a 'Reverse-O-Matic' transmission consisting of a flywheel mounted torque convertor, plus hydraulically activated forward and reverse multiple disc clutches, giving pedal operated instant forward and reverse.

The end of the two line policy in the USA also meant the virtual end of the Massey Harris lineage as far as tractors were concerned. Armed with the new Perkins engine facility at Peterborough, the trend was now towards diesel power in all models.

The first new model to appear was the MF-85 in 1959. This was available with a Continental 242 cu in gasoline engine, the same engine adapted to run on LPG, or a

Far left: The power plant for the MF-65.

57

A high clearance version of the MF-65.

Continental 276.5 cu in diesel. This model was renamed the 88 in 1960. In 1961 the Super 90 diesel replaced the 88. This machine had either Continental gasoline or LPG engines or a Perkins A4.300 diesel. The latter engine was the first specifically built for tractor use, with mountings cast into the

ris had a presence in France where Pony tractors had been assembled from the early postwar years. It was the French plant which was chosen to build the MF-25, viewed in some quarters as a replacement for the TE-20. This tractor had a Perkins 4.107 diesel of 3.125in bore and 3.5in

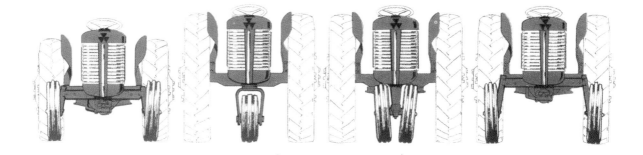

Like the Ferguson 40 alternative front axle configurations were available on the MF-65.

cylinder block, rather than bolted on. The A4.300 had a bore and stroke of 4.5 x 4.75in and developed 61/68hp at 2000rpm. The Super 90 was built until 1965.

One final line of development needs to be looked at before moving on. Massey Har-

stroke which gave 20/24hp at 2000rpm. This model was imported into the USA, but not the United Kingdom. The prototype of this model was a Fergie 20 fitted with a Perkins 4.99 engine, the 4.107 being a bored out version of the latter.

EXPERIMENTAL DESIGN

We now have to go back in time to discuss the introduction of a larger tractor with a totally new design of transmission, not allied to the 20/35 concept as the 65 was. It is well known that Harry Ferguson was opposed to large tractors, yet by 1950 he was beginning to realise that the only way into the growing world market was to build a bigger machine.

The experimental and design departments at Fletchamstead, Coventry, in anticipation of the forthcoming merger with Massey Harris, began work on a larger tractor. Some six prototypes were assembled between 1952 and 1956.

The engine was designed by Polish Engineer Alec Senkowski and was so arranged that it could have two, three, four or six cylinders and be built for petrol, diesel or TVO operation. About a dozen engine blocks were cast; it is not known how many were built up. Most of the extant photographs show a tractor with a petrol engine designated the 45C or the LTX. If volume production had been attained the tractor would have been designated the TE-60. After it was realised that the 45 engines would prove very expensive to produce, a Perkins L4 was tried in one of the tractors. The original TE-20 design showed weaknesses in the rear axle which were never overcome. The LTX used a double reduction rear axle design to reduce the load on the crown wheel and differential.

The LTX prototype tractor as restyled to match the FE-35.

Once Massey Harris had a hand in the affair the larger end of the market, was, in effect, covered by the 744 and 745 models. But as we have seen elsewhere these were not doing too well as far as sales were concerned.

The cost of putting the LTX into production was prohibitive, so Massey Ferguson, as it became in due course, looked elsewhere for a means of bringing a tractor to compete with the Fordson Major, Nuffield Universal Four and International BWD6, onto the UK market.

Left: The LTX or Ferguson 60 compared with a Fordson Major.

Below: The LTX compared with the Massey Harris 50.

The farmer was denied what would have been an excellent tractor, and had to wait a further two years until 1958 when until the MF-65 was launched. Everyone who experienced the LTX tractor at work stated what a superb performer it was. It is unfortunate that none of these prototypes have survived into preservation.

Ferguson 35/Massey Ferguson 35 built at Coventry

1956	1001	1960	171471	1964	352255
1957	9226	1961	220614	end	388382
1958	79553	1962	267528		
1959	125068	1963	307231		

First FE-35 built October 1956
First MF-35 (red/grey) built November 1957
Last Standard 23C engine, 166595
First Perkins 3-152 engine, serial number
166596, built November 1959
MF-35X introduced December 1962
(with Multipower)

Massey Ferguson 65 built at Coventry

1958	500001	1961	533180	1964	593028
1959	510451	1962	551733	end	614024
1960	520569	1963	552325		

First MF-65 Mark I built December 1957
First MF-65 Mark II introduced November 1960
First A4-203 engine 531453
Multipower introduced August 1962

Ferguson TO-20/TO-30 built by Harry Ferguson Inc. Detroit

1948	(Oct) 1	1951	39163	1954	125959
1949	1808	1952	72680	end	140000
1950	14660	1953	108645		

TO-30 built from serial number 60001 in August 1951

Ferguson TO-35 built by Massey Harris Ferguson Inc. Detroit

1954	140001	1956	167157
1955	140006	1957	171741

TO-35 Gas Deluxe

1958	178216	1960	203680
1959	188851	1961	207427

TO-35 Gas Special

1958	183348	1960	203198
1959	185504	1961	209484

TO-35 Diesel

1958	180742	1960	203360
1959	187719	1961	203680

Massey Ferguson MF-35 built by Massey Ferguson Inc. Detroit.

1960	204181	1962	222207
1961	211071	1963	235123

Ferguson 40 built by Massey Harris Ferguson Inc. Detroit.

1956	400001	1957	405671

Massey Harris 50 built by Massey Harris Ferguson Inc. Detroit

1955	500001	1957	510764
1956	500473	1958	515708

Following the cessation of the two line policy, F-40 and MH-50 tractors were assembled on the same production line, the model became the MF-50.

Massey Ferguson 50 built by Massey Ferguson Inc. Detroit

1959	522693	1961	528418	1963	533422
1960	528163	1962	529821	1964	536062

Massey Ferguson 65 built by Massey Ferguson Inc. Detroit.

1958	650001	1961	680210	1964	701057
1959	661164	1962	685370		
1960	671379	1963	693040		

Massey Ferguson 85 built by Massey Ferguson Inc.

1959	800001	1961	807750
1960	804355	1962	808564

Massey Ferguson 88 built by Massey Ferguson Inc.

1959	880001	1961	807750
1960	881453	1962	808564

Massey Ferguson 90 built by Massey Ferguson Inc.

1962	810000	1964	816113
1963	813170	1965	819342

Massey Ferguson 90WR built by Massey Ferguson Inc.

1962	885000	1963	886829
1963	885870	1964	888238

Ferguson and Massey Harris Ferguson Model Designations

TO-35   Detroit built tractor with Continental Z-134 engine, 1954-57.

FE-40   Detroit built tractor with Continental Z-134 engine, 1956-57, Ferguson.

MH-50   Detroit built tractor with Continental Z-134 engine, 1955-58, Massey.

FE-35   Standard built tractor with Standard engine, 1956-58.

MF-35   Standard/MF built tractor with Standard engine, 1958-59

MF-35   MF built tractor with Perkins 3.152 engine, 1959-62.

MF-35X   MF built tractor with Perkins A3-152 engine, 1962-64.

MF-65   MF built tractor with Perkins 4.192 engine, 1958-60.

MF-65   MkII MF built tractor with Perkins AD4.203 engine, 1958-65.

MF-25   MF French built tractor with Perkins 4.107 engine, 1963-65.

MF-88   MF Detroit built tractor with Continental diesel engine, 1960-1962.

MF Super 90   MF Detroit built tractor with Perkins A4.300 engine, 1961-1965.

35 SERIES ENGINE SPECIFICATIONS

Make and Model	Cyls	Bore and Stroke	CC	Fuel	HP	Used on
Cont. Z-134	4	3.3125in x 3.875in	2195	G	32.80	TO-35, F-40(5)
Perkins P3(TA)	3	3.5in x 5in	2360	D	34.00	Conversion pack.
Perkins P6(TA)	6	3.5in x 5in	4730	D	46.00	MH-744.
Perkins L4(TA)	4	4.25in x 4.75in	4420	D	50.00	MH-745
Standard	4	87mm x 92mm	2186	GG/K	34.00	FE-35, 135 petrol.
Standard 23C	4	84.14 x 101.6mm	2258	D	34.00	FE-35,
Perkins 4A-203	4	3.6in x 5in.	3335	D	55.50	MF-65
Perkins 3.152	3	3.6in x 5in.	2489	D	35.00	MF-35, 50 Perkins
A3-152	3	3.6in x 5in	2500	D	41.50	MF-35X, MF-50.
Perkins AD4-203	4	3.6in x 5in	3335	D	55.50	MF-65, 165.

The MF-35 fitted with a Ferguson mid-mounted mower.

Chapter Seven

PERKINS DIESELS

A Fordson N fitted with Perkins Leopard engine seen at the Royal Show, near Wolverhampton, in July 1937.

The Perkins P4 engine fitted to the Ford Ferguson 9N by Frank Perkins.

The acquisition of F Perkins Ltd gave MF the ability to produce their own engines for the first time, even Massey Harris prior to the merger had used bought in engines in the USA and Canada. It is worthwhile looking back and considering the history of Perkins Diesels as they were to have a profound effect on the development of Massey Ferguson tractors in the 1960s. The diesel engine had been around for some time in various forms, indeed its application in heavy goods vehicles and public service vehicles was becoming almost universal by 1945. Various attempts had been made to launch diesel tractors onto the UK market, but most of these had fallen by the wayside.

Strange to say there was not one totally new multi cylindered diesel on the British tractor scene pre-war. The Agricultural and General Engineers (AGE) tractors using Blackstone and Aveling engines were basically International 22/36 frames with diesel engines fitted. A few International petrol start diesels as fitted to their WD40 and TD35/40 Crawlers were imported, but like the domestic conversions they did not amount to much. Mainstay of the compression ignition picture was the Marshall, but even there production in total hardly got into four figures. As the majority of UK tractors were in any case multi cylinder units with automotive type engine and transmission layout, it was obvious that any manufacturer setting out to build tractor engines would adopt the multi-cylinder concept.

One of the immediate problems which arose in producing a diesel engine was its cost, not only in development terms, but in production also. Much finer tolerances were necessary and stronger components desirable to withstand the much greater compression pressures of such engines.

Barford & Perkins of Peterborough became part of Agricultural and General Engineers. Their main product line was motor road rolling equipment. The Peterborough works was closed by AGE when they took over in 1928/29 and their road-roller business was merged with that of Aveling & Porter to form Aveling-Barford.

Frank Perkins moved to Aveling's works at Strood as works manager. It was while he was there that the Vixen engine was designed, the drawings being done by a Short Brothers (Seaplanes) draughtsman working at weekends in the cellar of Mr Perkin's house. One or two engines were built at Avelings before the big decision was made to form a company to produce them.

Frank Perkins Ltd. was formed and premises at Queen Street, Peterborough, formerly occupied by Barford & Perkins, were rented. This was a case of coming

Much of Perkins early business was in supplying packs to enable existing types of tractors to be converted to diesel propulsion. The photographs on this page illustrate a Perkins conversion of a Ford 9N. The conversion meant that the bonnet was some 8 inches higher than normal.

The P4 engine used here was a Mark 1 version with internal inlet manifold.

The completed 9N conversion, with a plough attached.

The Massey Harris 744
prototype was a Canadian
built 44 fitted with a Perkins
P6(TA) engine.

The Perkins logo.

home. Frank Perkins obviously knew that the works were standing empty, and an approach to the owners, Milton Estates, secured a lease. Indeed quite a lot of equipment, such as the benches, were still there. Here the application of medium sized diesels for industrial and marine work in the 1930s, was pioneered. The Leopard, Wolf and Lynx engines were basically intended for multi use applications, covering vehicle, industrial and marine installations. However the use of the Leopard engine in tractors was instigated in the mid thirties. A Fordson N Land Utility tractor on Firestone wheels and tyres was supplied to F Perkins Ltd. on 11th February 1937 by the Willenhall, Staffordshire, Fordson dealer, Reginald Tildesley. This was serial number 808499 and it was delivered to Peterborough less engine.

A Perkins Leopard engine, serial number 7343, built on 16th June 1937 was fitted. This was a Leopard II engine with cast iron pistons and was rated at 34bhp at 1,100 rpm, it being derated from the usual industrial rating of 46bhp at 1500rpm to prevent damage to the rear axle.

The prototype tractor was tried out at Tettenhall near Wolverhampton in July 1937, prior to its exhibition at the Royal Show, which in 1937 was at the nearby Wrottesley Park.

In October and November 1937 a further 11 engineless tractors were supplied to Perkins by Tildesley, and in 1938/9 a further 17 arrived, making 29 in all. Incidentally, the TVO engines were used to provide a float for Tildesley's exchange engine scheme on the Fordson. The first Leopard conversion to go into full time farm service was bought by Mr T R C Blofeld of Hoverton Fruit Farms, Wroxham, Norfolk. It had the reputation of being a bad starter, but the early models had no self starter and were started on the handle using a decompressor. It would appear that most of the others were exported, and there is at least one extant in Australia and one in New Zealand. The latter example has a self starter. Another engine was also installed in a Muir Hill 3 cubic yard twin wheel dumper which appeared at the Public Works Exhibition at Olympia in London in 1938, this also had electric start.

With the advent of the war, conversion of tractors ceased, but in the meantime the development of a new range of engines was under way at Peterborough.

The result was the P series of engines which came onto the market in the early war years. From the outset, the design was very flexible. The engine could be built in three, four and six cylinder versions. These units used common parts saving much in development and production costs. Incidentally, one and two cylinder prototypes were built but never produced in any quantity and it took some time before the three cylinder variant appeared. One P3 prototype was built in 1939, and fitted in a London taxi, but it was to be 1951/2 before the engine was developed. The P series originally had names as had the other pre-war engines - the P6 was the Panther, the P4 the Puma and the P3 the Python. The P4 was introduced November 1937 and the P6 in February 1938. There were of course two versions of the P series. That for use in applications where engine speeds of over 1500rpm were required had aluminium alloy pistons, and that for use where engine speeds of below 1500rpm were required, had cast iron pistons. The calibration of the fuel injection pump produced engines with very different torque characteristics. The three, four and six cylinder variants, all shared the same bore and stroke of 3.5in x 5in. The swept volumes were P3 - 2.36 litres, P4 - 3.14 litres and P6 - 4.73 litres.

The design of the engines was such that different sumps, flywheel housings, front and side mounting plates and exhaust/inlet manifolds allowed a diversity of uses, whether with a wet clutch application such

Perkins most successful diesel engine conversions and supply for factory fitment in the late 1940s and early 1950s were P6(TA) engines to Ford for their Fordson Major (top) and P4(TA) engine to Nuffield for the DM4 (above).

as the Fordson Major, or a dry one such as the Massey Harris 744D. For vehicle use of course mountings were different, but the sump used with industrial applications had sufficient strength, when necessary, to include the engines in unit applications. There was even a petrol version of the P6, developed in conjunction with Dennis Brothers of Guildford, to replace their equivalent petrol engine, though only two of these experimental engines were built.

The P series had not been used widely in tractors until Frank Perkins converted a Fordson Major for his own use. The result

A Perkins P3(TA) engined Fergie 20 fitted with Tracpak crawler conversion produced by a firm in Leeds.

was that Ford Motor Company sent two Majors for conversion, one with a P4, and the other a P6. Both had fabricated sumps and flywheel housings. Whilst both gave a satisfactory performance, the P6 was chosen due to its lower maximum speed which suited the E27N gearbox better. Ford adopted the engine as a production option it also must be remembered that the Ford dealer network were already geared up for Perkins spares and service as the engine in its vehicle (V) form was fitted in the Ford Thames lorry.

So it came to pass that the P6(TA) engine was born and graced a good few thousand E27Ns, either straight off the production line or in the form of conversion packs which Perkins sold themselves.

Morris Motors were also looking for a diesel to fit in their new Nuffield Universal tractor. They chose the P4(TA) which fitted the Nuffield chassis more easily than the P6 fitted the E27N. In the case of the Fordson a special sump had to be cast to support both the front axle and connect this with the flywheel housing. Whilst most P series engines were made for dry clutches, the E27N's wet clutch also required a special flywheel housing and suitable oil seal for the starter motor.

As we shall see in due course, other manufacturers made use of the Perkins engines in their TA (tractor adapted) form.

One feature of the adoption of Perkins units in some applications was the fact that the power output of the engine was much more than the equivalent petrol or TVO models. In addition the initial cost of the diesel engined version was greater than the equivalent spark ignition one.

With Ford and Nuffield offering Perkins engined variants, and David Brown their own engine, it was not long before Ferguson's sales force were calling for a diesel version of the TE-20. Now as Harry Ferguson himself was not a diesel fan, it took some considerable persuasion to get him to agree to a diesel engined tractor at all.

The Perkins P3 was looked at, but the cost of installation and the modifications needed would not suit, so a Standard engine was fitted instead. This engine was designed by Freeman-Sanders specifically for Ferguson, and was built for them by the Standard Motor Company, who later developed the same unit for use in their Vanguard car.

There was one thing which opened the way for a conversion pack from Perkins for the Fergie 20 and that was the fact that the diesel engine supplied by Ferguson could not be fitted to existing tractors. The first tractor converted by Perkins was actually a

Ford-Ferguson 9NAN for his own use, but the principles of the conversion were the same for the TE-20. The 9NAN was acquired by Frank Perkins during the war and the engine fitted in this case was a P4, there being no P3s at that time. It was cut up in the mid 1970s under Customs supervision, along with an MF-85 imported as a test tractor for the A4-300 engine, as no import duty had been paid on them!

After the war, Massey Harris were looking at building tractors in the UK, where they saw great export potential. At that time the government was supporting the ground

Left and bottom: *Two views of the P3(TA) engine as adapted for the TE-20 conversion pack.*

Perkins pulling power on a Cambridgeshire farm with P3, P4 and P6 engines fitted to the tractors in the picture..

nut scheme in Africa (see Glossary). A few type 44 frames were taken and fitted with the P6(TA) engine. Tractor assembly commenced at Manchester in 1948 but to due to shortage of space, assembly of the 744, as it became, was moved to Kilmarnock in Scotland, from 1949.

Thus, not only were Perkins engines now being fitted in production by leading manufacturers, they were also available to convert spark ignition engined units to diesel. By the late forties conversion packs were available to convert most of the popular models.

The promotion of diesel conversion packs was just as well, as new engine busi-

A now preserved typical example of a Fergie 20 converted to diesel using the Perkins P3(TA) conversion pack.

A Fergie TE-20 P3(TA) conversion about to be demonstrated. The Dodge Kew lorry is equipped with a P6(V) engine.

ness fell off considerably with Ford fitting their own diesel to the new Fordson Major, and Nuffield fitting the BMC engine to the Universal by the early fifties.

The P series was not without its problems in agricultural service. Unlike many road hauliers and others who used the V (vehicle) version, farmers were not renowned for their care and attention to machinery, and a diesel engine requires more of this to maintain peak performance. The chain driven timing could, if not properly adjusted,

make starting difficult, and early tractor applications had engine breather problems later cured by modification. The tendency to over-rev the P series (TA) units with their cast iron pistons often caused bent conrods, little end and cylinder head gasket failures. Indeed later P6 engines all had alloy pistons which alleviated many of the problems, and many rebuilds received these also. This is why a lot of P6(TA) engines still extant appear to the unknowing to be 'V' or vehicle ones! The main problem with the P6(TA) was the farmer's habit of leaving the engines running when not working, as they were used to doing with paraffin engines. This caused the exhaust ports to choke with carbon. An acquaintance of mine who serviced such machines once told me that he had taken off manifolds to see ports with holes not large enough to push a pencil through. Of all the tractors fitted with the P6(TA), the Fordson Major E27N was the most successful. Early models had the habit of breaking halfshafts, however a new design with suitable heat treatment cured this, and the E27N

speeds up to 2000rpm. It had a bore and stroke of 4.25 x 4.75in, a swept volume of 4.42 litres and could be set to give up to 59bhp at 2000rpm. A gear driven timing arrangement was fitted and the camshaft, unlike the P series, was in the normal position with push rod operation of the valves. The cylinder liners were, however, of the wet type.

The new engine was adopted by various manufacturers for use in tractors. The Massey Harris 745 used the L4(TA) from 1953 and M-H also adopted it for use in their combines. It was also available as a

A Fergie 20 fitted with Perkins 4.99 engine as a development tractor for the French built MF-25.

back end was really the only one which could stand the full power of the P6. This was the tractor which has endeared the P6(TA) to present day collectors and enthusiasts above all other. Of course more were built than any other diesel engined tractor of the era.

1953 saw the introduction of a completely new engine for industrial use, the L4. This unit was designed expressly for low

conversion for older Fordson Majors, the current Fordson Major and Nuffields. A3.152 engines supplied to Ferguson's Detroit plant were fitted to MF-35s and also MF-50s. The Dieselmatic 65 used the 4A.203 engine in the USA, and later the AD4.203, whilst the Super 90, only built in the western hemisphere, used the A4.300. This engine was a bit more than just a bored out 4-270. It had a dedicated tractor block,

with cast-in tractor fittings, dry type cylinder liners, a five bearing crankshaft and a harmonic balancer unit.

The 4.270 was an update on the old L4 and brought direct injection to this engine, plus the use of a distributor type fuel injection pump. Conversion packs for the older tractors now used this engine instead of the L4 and other manufacturers such as Marshall also now took the newer engine instead.

Allis Chalmers had fitted Perkins P3 engines in their model B at their Totton, Southampton plant, and continued to use Perkins engines, the P3.144 in their D270 and D272 models, once assembly had moved to Essendine. The ED40 tractor used a Standard Motor Company 23C engine however. This was a tactic used by Standard to annoy Perkins and M-F. They sold these engines at lower prices to make up for the loss of production encountered when M-F ceased taking these engines following their acquisition of Perkins. They also made sales to Ford by supplying a limited number of petrol 87mm engines for Dextas sold in Denmark and elsewhere. These latter were, however, of special build to suit the Dexta gearbox housing.

A Beauvais (France) built MF-25 vineyard model with Perkins 4.99 engine.

Small numbers of Perkins engines were supplied to other manufacturers both at home and abroad, examples of some of these are shown elsewhere in the book. Notable crawlers which used Perkins engines were the Howard Platypus, the Bristol and the French built Continental.

As the sixties progressed and the seventies dawned an even greater variety of products came out of Peterborough and a new

MASSEY HARRIS BEFORE AND AFTER THE MERGER

Massey Harris were well enough known in the United Kingdom prior to the Second World War but more for their implements, especially binders. A number of tractors were sold in the UK prior to 1939 and others came over under the wartime lend-lease scheme.

In 1947 a new range was introduced in the USA and Canada, based very much on what it replaced but with smaller and larger models added.

The smallest tractor was the No 11 Pony, designed for market garden work. Next came the No 20, a two furrow tractor available in both standard and rowcrop forms. This became the 22 in 1948. The 30 was a 2/3 furrow tractor, and the 44, which was the most popular and successful of all these models, was of three furrow capacity. The 55 at the top of the range was of 4/5 furrow capacity and available only as a standard tractor. This model was never successful having a succession of engine and gearbox faults which did not help sales. Both the 44 and 55 were sold in Britain.

The British government's infamous and costly scheme to encourage the growing of ground nuts in its African colonies was responsible for MH building tractors in the UK, as in 1947 they obtained a contract to supply tractors and implements for the scheme. It was found that the Perkins P6 (TA) engine would fit the 44 frame and the transmission and rear axle would be imported. Any other parts required could be bought in from UK suppliers. Only 16 machines had been actually produced at MH's Manchester plant when, due to government pressure and lack of space, tractor assembly was transferred to Kilmarnock in 1949. Whilst the intention was to export most 744s, it failed miserably on the UK market where in 1952 only 68 were sold as opposed to the 5225 exported.

In 1953 tractors built numbered 2546 and the 744 was discontinued. It was replaced in 1954 by the 745 with the recently introduced Perkins L4 engine and an improved lift, supplied by Adriolic of Milngavie in Scotland. It continued in production, albeit spasmodically, until 1958. Towards the end of production the supply of cast frames dried up and a new model, the 745, was developed which incorporated channel side frames.

Massey Harris persevered with their own line over this period, the basic models being the same as in the late forties with some updating. The 22 series were renamed the Colt and Mustang; the Pony and Pacer models were added, and diesel engines were offered on the 33, 44 and 55 models.

In the two years before the merger, the MH range was redesigned, the 33 becoming the 333, the 44 the 444 and the 55 the 555, with little change in specification. A 'live' PTO was offered on these late models.

So the MH line ended. The last true Massey Harris models faded into obscurity with the end of the two line policy in 1958, all future models being based on Ferguson ancestry. The links with Perkins however did develop the relationship which was to result in that concern's purchase by M-H-F.

The former Massey Harris factory at Kilmarnock was turned over to manufacture of implements for MF tractors although combine harvester production also continued there. Sadly the factory is now but a memory having been demolished in the 1990s.

Top: The Massey Harris 745 was the last Massey Harris model to be built in the UK.

Above: Massey Harris could never complete on price with the likes of the Fordson Major seen here along with a 744. In 1948 a Fordson E27N cost £281 with TVO and £550 with P6 engine and the 744 cost £925.

Chapter Eight

WORLDWIDE MARKETS

The smallest tractor in the new 100 range was the French built 130.

The 130 was, in effect, an updated Ferguson 25/825 with new styling.

B y the early sixties, it can now be seen that there was a certain amount of standardisation in the MF tractors built in both the eastern and western hemispheres, unlike Ford, for example, whose designs in England and the USA were totally different.

With the trend towards unified product lines moving ahead in all automotive fields, MF took the step to introduce a completely new range of models in 1965, with unified styling and specifications worldwide. The demand for gasoline engines was still evident in the USA and thus Continental engines still appeared in these tractors.

The new models were really developments of the MF-35/65 family, a fact that simplified changes to the production facilities. Not all the range were produced at all three assembly plants. Whilst mechanical specifications were improved, the visual impact of the changes came in the styling and new tinwork which gave all the models in the range a standard appearance.

The MF-135 replaced the 35, the MF-150 the MF-50 (available only in the Western hemisphere), and the 165 the 65. In fact these models bore a similar relationship to each other as the 35-50-65 did. The use of Perkins engines saw the MF-135 and MF-150 fitted with the AD3.152 engine. The MF-165 had the AD4.203 of its predecessor. Whilst Continental engines were still available in all these models, the Z134 in the 135 Special, the Z145 in the MF-135 Deluxe and MF-150, and the G176 in the MF-165, petrol versions of the Perkins engines were developed and the later MF-135/MF-150 became available with the Perkins AG3.152 engine and the 165 with the AG4.212. Six forward speeds were provided in all models along with two reverse, but the equipping of any model with Multipower doubled those. The 135 retained the beam type front axle of its predecessor, whilst the other models had the usual arrangement to allow the use of rowcrop type equipment. The new styling gave all the models the new more square appearance.

The 175 was a new model, and featured a Perkins 4.236 engine. This was designed specially to fit the tractor, and was the first Perkins engine to feature the inlet and exhaust manifolds on the same side.

Indeed, when the 165 was updated in 1968, the old style AD4.203 engine had given way to a new unit based on the 4.236 but with shorter stroke, the 4.212. The American built 180 was similar but designed for rowcrop work.

Hydraulics on all models except the 130 were improved, with the addition of 'pressure control' which allowed draft control to be used with trailing implements. One feature of all models, apart from the 130, was the use of many common transmission components. There were detail differences between Detroit and Coventry built tractors, those for Britain and certain other European territories having the lamps recessed into the front grille, whilst those for America and elsewhere initially had the lights mounted to the side of the radiator grille. The advent of flat topped fenders removed the lights of tractors for the western hemisphere into neat fairings in front of those fenders.

In 1971 the 175 was replaced by the 178 with a larger engine, the Perkins A4.248.

In November 1971, in time for the UK's

Direct successor to the Fergie 20 was the 135, the British built diesel engined version is seen here.

major agricultural event, the Smithfield Show in London, the 100 series was expanded to cover six models. These consisted of the three models of the basic range, with different option packages such as no Multipower, manual steering or 'live' PTO, to meet the requirements of export markets. The 135 and 165 continued as before, whilst the 178 had been replaced by

Above and right: *A few 135s were built with Standard petrol engines for use at show jumping events where noise needed to be kept at a minimum. The advertising potential of such units was immense.*

the 185 earlier in the same year. The basic range was very price competitive for those customers who did not want too much sophistication. The above did not feature gearbox spacers (see below).

The first cabs made available for the 100 series were not safety cabs, indeed they were constructed of fibreglass. The first safety cabs were of composite construction with canvas (plastic) infill, and the option of engine side shrouds which diverted engine heat to warm the cab. From 1971 the option of a rigid clad type cab was available at extra cost. In due course full safety cabs to 'Q' specification had to be supplied for tractors used in Great Britain, but as the 100 series were being produced mainly for overseas markets by the mid seventies, it was often the case that domestic sales received proprietary cabs.

One of the problems when a cab was fit-

ted was the restricted access to the driving position. This was overcome by introducing a spacer on the 100 series 'Super Spec' tractors from late 1971, which fitted between the gearbox and rear axle and lengthened the wheelbase of the tractor. This allowed the fitting of a more spacious safety cab. It also altered the weight distribution of the tractor to its advantage, allowing the attachment and use of heavier implements without the need for front weights. With these improvements, including the use of spacers, the 135 became the 148, the 165 became the 168, the 135 the 148, and a stretched version of the 185, the 188, was also introduced, in time for the Smithfield Show in 1971, where the improved range were shown. The 'Super-Spec' tractors also had independent PTO, Multi-Power transmission, spring suspension seat, high capacity hydraulic pump, and in the case of the 188 only, power steering and power adjusted wheel track.

In practice the range of models was complicated by the fact that if a customer desired he could up-grade a basic model or down grade a 'Super-Spec' model. Where

Multi-Power was not specified a new eight speed gearbox was offered on all models except the 135 and 165 which still used a six speed unit.

The spacer idea was also put to good use in that the extra room it provided could be used to fit an optional 'creeper' gearbox in place of the spacer. As far as normal gearboxes were concerned, the 130 had an eight speed gearbox within high and low ratios, whilst the other models had a basic six speed transmission over high and low ratios, which became 12 with the application of Multipower, which was optional.

The smallest model sold in the UK was the 130, which was an update of the MF-30 built in France, with a Perkins 4.107 four cylinder diesel. On the other hand, the largest conventional tractor available on world markets was the US built 1100, fitted with the Perkins A6.354 diesel or a Waukesha F320-G six cylinder petrol engine. This became the 1130 when fitted with a turbocharged version of the diesel engine, the Perkins AT6.354. The 1080 was a relative, but this had a Perkins 4.318 diesel. This tractor was derived from the US built 180 and was also assembled in France. The ultimate in 100 series power was the 1150 built at the Detroit plant from 1970-72, which featured a Perkins V8.510 diesel. At the other end of the scale, the French plant specialised in the vineyard (vigneron) and orchard (etroit) models based on the 130 and 135 tractors. By using derated and uprated engines 122, 140 and 145 models were offered, the 122 vigneron having a 4.99 rather than the 4.107 engine of the 130, and the 140 and 145 engines used the 3.152 engine set to run at 2150 rpm and 2250 rpm respectively rather than the standard 2000 rpm.

The 135 in basic form following the introduction of square topped fenders.

Later 135 tractors had a revised front axle design.

This is a 135s with spacer fitted to lengthen the wheelbase.

The 165 was the replacement for the 135; later examples had an improved engine, the 4.212, as used on this example.

Two views of the 175, the largest tractor in the range sold in the UK at the time of its introduction in 1965. Improved features were added to this model in the early 1970s.

Top right: The 135 with original style of glass fibre cab.

Right: The 1100 was introduced in 1965 in the USA but was first seen in the United Kingdom at the 1967 Smithfield Show.

Centre and right: The 100 series with the first generation of safety cabs. These cabs were steel framed with flexible cladding and incorporated a cab heating system using the side screens shown.

The 168 was one of the 'Super-Spec' tractors introduced in 1971. Note the gearbox spacer and spring suspension seat.

'MULTI-POWER'

But what is Multi-Power and how does it work? A little diversion to discuss gearboxes first though. In the late 1940s and 1950s when it was realised that the tractor was a far more versatile beast than anyone ever imagined twenty years previously, the need to provide a range of working speeds other than the normal 3-4 forward and one reverse gears arose.

There were various ways of achieving this. With a single range gearbox as used in Ferguson models up to the 35, the more speeds you add the more complex it becomes. The route taken by most manufacturers was to create a dual range gearbox where one or even two secondary units gave two or even three alternatives; when compounded with the main gearbox it was possible to double or even treble the number of gears available The first MF tractor to have this feature was the 35.

When it came to the Ford Fergie and Fergie 20, Howard of Bedford provided a reduction gearbox for these machines. This was built in to the transmission and was a secondary unit.

Multi-Power was developed from the shuttle transmission fitted by Ferguson in the USA to industrial tractors. Here, allied to a torque convertor, the gearbox simply consisted of two planetary units one for forward motion and one for reverse. Two pedals provided directional control, which was hydraulic.

Multi-Power was also hydraulically controlled. The need to contain the additional gears within the existing transmission was solved in a unique way. There were two sets of primary gears at the front of the gearbox. One set were in constant mesh and the other set were engaged by means of a hydraulic clutch. Now you may ask, if the second set was engaged would not the whole transmission lock solid. But no! A freewheel device was incorporated in the driven gear of the constant mesh set and as the lower shaft was being driven faster when the second set was engaged hydraulically, this came into operation and overrode the first set. The system's one disadvantage however was that on over-run, engine braking was lost, when in low ratio.

Ford introduced a similar, shift on the go, transmission system in 1958. Called, Select-o-Speed, it met with some success in the United States but was not popular in Great Britain.

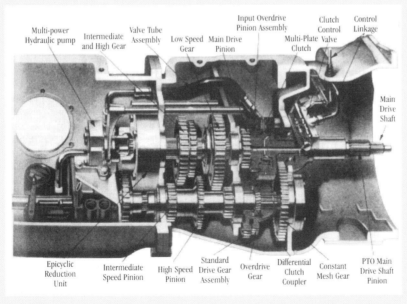

The illustrations on this page feature the MF-135 range sold in the western hemisphere.

Top: The 135 Special was available with a Perkins AG3.152 gasoline engine and six speed transmission.

Above: The orchard model was also equipped with the Perkins A3.152 diesel engine. It was only 49in in height to the top of the steering wheel.

Right: A rear view of the vineyard model.

Left: The 135 Standard offered the usual choice of a Perkins A3.152 diesel or AG3.152 gasoline engine and the option of either eight or twelve speed Multi-Power transmissions.

Top: An illustration from a sales brochure for an early model of the Detroit built 165 series showing the different lighting arrangements which were required for the United States market.

Above: The MF-180 was designed expressly for the North American market. Although available with a conventional four wheeled layout, the most popular version was that with the vee twin front wheels for rowcrop work. This model had an adjustable steering column and a flat floor which enabled the operator to stand up or sit down whilst driving the machine.

100 Series, built at Banner Lane, Coventry.

Massey Ferguson 135

1965	101	1968	93305	1971	162200
1966	30283	1969	117429		
1967	67597	1970	141426		

Massey Ferguson 135 updated

1971	400001	1975	445602	1979	487350
1972	403518	1976	457866	end	490714
1973	419583	1977	469335		
1974	432709	1978	479192		

Massey Ferguson 165

1965	500001	1968	547384	1971	597745
1966	512207	1969	563701		
1967	530825	1970	581457		

Massey Ferguson 165 updated

1971	100001	1974	126448	1977	155687
1972	103622	1975	135036	1978	164417
1973	116353	1976	145432	1979	173144
				end	173696

Massey Ferguson 175 (178 from 1968)

1965	700001	1968	722679	1971	747283
1966	705652	1969	732158	1972	753108
1967	714166	1970	740301		

Massey Ferguson 175 S

1968	650000	1970	653721	1972	657362
1969	652061	1971	656011		

Massey Ferguson 148

1972	600001	1975	605578	1978	609969
1973	602153	1976	607701	1979	610893
1974	604449	1977	609159	end	610982

Massey Ferguson 168

1971	250001	1974	254307	1977	259959
1972	250005	1975	255967	1978	260617
1973	252121	1976	258064	1979	261103
				end	261173

Massey Ferguson 185

1971	300001	1974	315219	1977	332107
1972	302833	1975	319923	1978	335211
1973	310398	1976	326109	1979	339755
				end	340096

Massey Ferguson 188

1971	350001	1974	357063	1977	368350
1972	350006	1975	360784	1978	370156
1973	353296	1976	365087	1979	371306
				end	371333

100 Series, built in the USA, 1964-1966.

Massey Ferguson 135

1964	641000001	1966	641014871
1965	641001909		

Massey Ferguson 150

1964	642000001	1966	631000505
1965	642000015		

Massey Ferguson 165

1964	643000001	1966	643000149
1965	643000003		

Massey Ferguson 175

1964	644000001	1966	644000214
1965	644000004		

Massey Ferguson 180

1964	645000001	1966	647000047
1965	645000002		

100 Series, built in USA, 1967-1969.

A common serial number sequence was used for the 150, 165, 175 and 180 tractors.

1967	9A10001	1969	9A63158
1968	9A39836		

1000 Series, built in the USA, 1964-1966.

Massey Ferguson 1100

1964	650000001	1966	650000831
1965	650000003		

Massey Ferguson 1130

1964	650500001	1966	651500049
1965	650500004		

1000 Series, built 1967-1969.

A common serial number sequence was used for the 1100, 1130 and 1080 tractors.

1967	9B10001	1969	9B18673.
1968	9B14693		

100 SERIES ENGINE SPECIFICATIONS

Make and Model	Cyls	Bore and Stroke	CC	Fuel	HP	Used on
Perkins A3-152	3	3.6in x 5in	2500	D	41.50	MF-135
Perkins AD4-203	4	3.6in x 5in	3335	D	55.50	MF-165.
Cont. G 176	4	3.58in x 4.38in	2883	G	46.92	MF-165
Cont. Z 145	4	3.375in x 4.062in	2376	G	35.36	MF-135 D/L, MF-150
Perkins AG3.152	3	3.6in x 5in	2489	G	35.00	Late MF-135/ MF-150
Perkins AG4.212	4	3.875in x 4.5in	3472	G	55.00	MF-165.
Perkins A4.212	4	3.875in x 4.5in	3472	D	58.30	late MF-165.
Perkins A4.236	4	3.875in x 5in	3865	D	63.34	MF-175/168.
Perkins A4.248	4	3.980in x 5in	4062	D	68.00	MF-178/185/188
Perkins A4.300	4	4.5in x 4.75in	4950	D	68.00	MF Super 90.
Cont. G 206	4	3.9in x 4.5in	3374	G	62.33	MF-175, MF-180
Perkins AG4.236	4	3.875in x 5in	3865	G	62.00	MF-175, MF-180
Perkins 4.107	4	3.125in x 3.5in	1752	D	26.96	MF-825, MF-130.
Perkins A6.354	6	3.875in x 5in	5798	D	93.94	MF-1100
Perkins AT6.354	6	3.875in x 5in	5798	TD	120.51	MF-1130
Perkins A4.318	4	4.5in x 5in	3185	D	81.96	MF-1080
Waukesha F320-G	6	4.125in x 4in	5341	G	90.29	MF-1100

100 series tractors posed with the MF-1200 four wheel drive, a Massey Harris four wheel drive from the 1920s, a Fergie 20 and a Massey Harris Pony.

Chapter Nine

THE COMPETITION

The David Brown Cropmaster was similar in size and power to the Ferguson TE-20. DB scored a first by producing the first diesel model with an in house built engine in 1949.

David Brown moved from the light to the heavy end of the market in 1956 when they launched the 900 with its 40 bhp engine.

Until the Ferguson TE-20 entered the UK market in 1946 the tractor market in the United Kingdom was dominated by the Ford Motor Company. The Fordson N, better known to many, as the Standard Fordson remained in production during the 1939-45 period when up to 100 units a day were being produced. A replacement for this model had been planned as early as 1938. When the Fordson Major first saw the light of day in 1945 Britain was still at war. All tractors supplied to farmers were subject to supply under a War Agricultural Committee permit. Under these arrangements no competition was allowed, in any case Fordson production accounted for the supply of over 90% of all tractors in the United Kingdom from 1939 to 1945.

What other manufacturers did was minimal, and the balance was made up by the import of various US makes and models of tractor. Only in special cases could one get a permit to have anything other than a Fordson. There had been a limited number of Ford Ferguson 9Ns imported into the United Kingdom, some figures quoted suggesting as many as 50,000 are vastly exaggerated. Most of these tractors were allocated to farmers with a need for cultivation and rowcrop work.

Enter the politicians. The 1945 Labour government's policy was one of export, export, export, to earn much needed dollars for the repayment of wartime loans. Ford struggled on with a clapped out production line and only half the tractor they had wanted to produce after the war, due to the fact that they could not get material permits to import the machine tools necessary to build a new engine.

Whilst Ford lost out, the need for full employment meant that others, including Ferguson, were moved into direct competition with the very outfit that had served Britain so well in the war years.

But others were in the market place. David Brown's production capacity had never been a major threat to Ford and their production of agricultural machines was very restricted during wartime. Once the peace had been won, they set out improving their models with the eventual introduction of the VAK1C Cropmaster in 1947. Whilst production never reached more than 7,000 units a year, every one sold was a loss to Ford and one less E27N built. The Cropmaster had many more modern features including a six speed gearbox, an up-to-date overhead valve engine and coil ignition. Despite the lack of the Ferguson System, three point linkage was available on David Brown's postwar models.

The contribution of Marshalls of Gainsborough to the pre-war tractor output was minimal, but they moved into a post-

A return to a smaller model came in 1960 with the introduction of the David Brown 850 rated at 25hp.

This view taken at Ford's Dagenham plant shows lines of New Fordson Majors in early 1952. This tractor was possibly Ford's most successful model and was produced with improvements for the next 11 years.

war world with big ideas. The new Field Marshall had its sights set, in the eyes of the Marshall sales boys at least, on taking on the big players. Improved the Field Marshall Series One and Two models may have been over the old model M, but sales were still mostly to their old customers, mainly contractors and threshermen. There was no serious competition to Ferguson from this front.

There were of course still a trickle of imports from the USA; John Deere, Case, Allis Chalmers and Oliver provided a few units in the late forties until import tariffs forced them to either abandon the market or seek a production facility in the United Kingdom. John Deere tried and failed when politics intervened. The new Conservative government in 1951 cut off subsidies for those who wanted to set up in the UK. They went to Germany instead and it was to be the end of the decade before John Deere would become a threat again.

Allis Chalmers, International, and Massey

International introduced a completely new model in 1956. The B250 was built at the old Jowett plant at Bradford in Yorkshire.

Harris had a stronger presence in the UK than other American firms. All set up production facilities in Britain in the late 1940s, with government aid. Allis Chalmers opted to build a version of their B tractor at Totton near Southampton. This unit was never a real challenge to Ford being in the lower horsepower class and of a design not really suited to the needs of most British farmers. Nor was it any threat to Ferguson as sheer volume of production at Banner Lane saw to that! Now if A-C had built their U model in Britain that would have been another story. The last examples of this august type reached British shores in 1949 and thereafter Allis had no real chance of attacking Ford sales.

International had always been a strong contender for a slice of the UK market, and provided the first real challenger to the E27N in the form of their Farmall M, built at Doncaster from 1949. This tractor had all the features of the E27N but with a vastly superior engine and gearbox. The one weakness of the M and strength of the E27N were their hydraulic systems. Ford went out from the beginning to provide a good lift with three point linkage, albeit without the

Ferguson System, whilst International played around with half baked modifications to their rockshaft lift as fitted to US built tractors. Nevertheless, in the ten years from 1949 to 1959, International provided nearly 40,000 units. Whilst they could produce nearly twice as many tractors as David Brown, it was still a drop in the ocean if you think that in 1948 over 50,000 E27Ns and 57,000 TE-20s were built.

Massey Harris sold few tractors in the UK where they were mainly known for machinery. However, the ground nut scheme saw the launch of their 744; a 44 frame and transmission fitted with a Perkins P6(TA) engine. Needless to say the E27N with the same engine fitted was a far superior machine and Massey Harris had to be content with those pickings which one always gets from the minority of customers who will not go along with the masses.

The biggest problem, as far as the sales department as Dagenham was concerned, was always Harry Ferguson. Outside interference at the beginning of the war had caused unnecessary tensions between Detroit and Percival Perry, head of Ford UK. Much as it would have been desirable to see the Ford 9N built at Dagenham, by the time the idea was mooted, Britain was at war with Germany, and there was no way that the materials and tooling could have been released for the introduction of a new model.

It was just as well Ford UK never became involved for by the time the war had ended Ferguson had broken with Ford in the USA and was wooing others in the USA and the UK with a view to having his tractor built. The biggest kick in the teeth for Ford was the way in which government money was used to provide a brand new production facility for Ferguson at Banner Lane in Coventry. The Ford salesmen soon dubbed

The International B275 replaced the B250 in 1958 and featured a more powerful engine and ten speed gearbox.

The International B414 came in 1961 with more improvements and new styling

85

BMC reduced the size of their Nuffield Universal by fitting a three cylinder engine to create the Universal Three, seen in these front and rear views, in 1957.

Although intended to be a direct competitor to the Ferguson the rear view of the Nuffield Universal Three retained many parts from the larger Universal Four as can be seen in this rear view.

this competition, 'The Grey Menace'. They had to fight hard to counter this throughout the 1950s. An early advantage for Ford was that the original Fergie only offered a petrol engine, but soon the TED-20 appeared and closed that gap. It was often the case that once a farmer had bought and used a Ferguson, he was hooked and it was difficult, if not impossible for a dealer with another tractor, to persuade him to change.

Enter the Nuffield Universal. Available from the outset in petrol, diesel, and TVO forms it had been well known since 1946 that this machine was under development. It is said that one of the reasons for Ford going diesel was the threat from Nuffield. Both of course used bought in Perkins engines. This tractor and the Fordson Major were considered to cater for the heavy end of the market, whilst the Fergie 20 introduced a new concept to the light end. Nuffield production figures for the period are not available, but going by later ones, they only took a small slice of the market.

One tractor which proved to be a non starter in the competition stakes was the grandly named, Yeoman of England, introduced in 1949 by the Staffordshire firm, Turners. Plagued by problems from start to finish it only took the eventual arrival of the new Fordson Major in 1952 to kill off this and other models, such as the Marshall.

WAC permits continued to be required for the purchase of new tractors until 1948/9. With the emphasis on exports, 50% of the production of all makes was exported in the late forties, shortages were still evident in the UK market place. It was very much a case of whichever salesman could get you a tractor first got the business. There were of course plenty of ex War Agricultural Committee and military surplus Fordsons coming into the market place. These sources very often brought a tractor for the first time onto a small farm where horses had reigned supreme until then. This means of supply had little effect

Allis Chalmers updated their model B in the United Kingdom offering Perkins diesel power as an option.

The final direct descendant of the Allis Chalmers model B was the D272

on Ferguson's plans as the availability of any tractor was welcome in the 1945-50 period. In those postwar years many sales were to customers who were having their first tractor on the farm. The market was thus expanding as the new Fergie range arrived on the scene. The number of horses employed on the land was to decline rapidly in the years after 1950.

It always seemed that the Dagenham boys had their hands tied behind their backs in the immediate postwar period. Ferguson's ability to built up to 300 units a day was an immediate threat. The Fordson Major, by sheer volume of production, put many of Britain's farms back into shape in those still austere years from 1945 to 1950, but the Ferguson System played its role in changing the whole concept of mechanised farming. Much as it would have been desirable to have a new Fordson model earlier, when it did come, the new Fordson Major was just the machine to take the heavy end of the market by storm - after all nobody

Ford produced a plethora of variants of its basic Jubilee design introduced in 1953 until the worldwide range came in 1964. This is a mid 1950s rowcrop variant. The Jubilee model NAA was so named as it was launched in the year of Ford's 50th anniversary.

could build tractors in the quantity that Ford could, and at the price! Ford also benefited from having a good dealer network and a ready availability of spare parts.

As can be seen, most of the competition was no real threat to Ferguson once the Fergie 20 had proved itself. But with the expiry of patent rights real competition was to appear. There had been a plethora of small tractors appearing on the UK market in the late 1940s, the BMB President, the OTA, the Newman and suchlike but these units were but a drop in the ocean. In the USA the Ford 8N was Ferguson's greatest worry but in the UK nothing posed a real threat to the Fergie until the mid 1950s. Whilst Allis Chalmers had updated their model B to suit UK conditions, with a series of models ending in the ED40, the move by Ford into the light end of the market posed the first real major challenge to the Ferguson's supremacy. Nuffield brought their challenge in with the Universal Three in 1957 almost at the same time as the Ford Dexta appeared. International were the other major contender when they launched the B250 in 1956, and David Brown continued improvements to their models with the 25 and 30 series of the early 1950s, gradually moving the range towards the heavy end of the market with the 900 series launched in 1956.

The move by Massey Ferguson into the heavy area with the 65 was to even things out. Thereafter most major manufacturers tended to develop and offer a range of models. It was Ford's move to four models in 1964 with the 2000, 3000, 4000 and 5000 which had a direct influence on Massey Ferguson's Red Giant range of 130, 135, 165 and 175 machines.

It only remains to study the tables which follow to see just how production and competition moved from the single models of the 1940s to the greater choice of the 1960s which led in turn to the vast choice available as the twenty first century dawns.

UK PRODUCTION OF FORDSON/ FERGUSON TRACTORS 1946-60

Year	Fordson	Ferguson
1946	25489	315
1947	35116	20578
1948	50563	56877
1949	33578	38688
1950	42335	51374
1951	35965	73498
1952	30177	69443
1953	29576	57218
1954	45689	60093
1955	48872	60485
1956	41011	38297
1957	45965	70326

	High	Low	High	Low
1958	35986	22414	10449	45514
1959	43435	21874	10117	46402
1960	46013	27489	12610	49142

US PRODUCTION OF FORD/FERGUSON TRACTORS 1947-56

Year	Ford	Ferguson
1947	37908	38932*
1948	103462	1808
1949	104267	12852
1950	97956	24503
1951	98442	33517
1952	4930 ^	35965
1953	72568	17314
1954	10615 ^	14047
1955	66656	27151
1956	39097	25963+

Notes: * Built by Ford Motor Co.
^ Part production only.
1952 shows 8N only, 1954 shows NAA only.
Cutoff figure for new model not known.
+ Consists of 4584 TO35, 5671 F40 and 15708 MH50.

OTHER PLAYERS

It wasn't until the 1960s that M-F models really unique to France were produced. This is the 155 which featured the 165 transmission allied to a three cylinder engine.

The Beauvais plant specialised in vineyard tractors. This is a 135 vigneron with safety frame.

Right from the beginning, there were problems in exporting Ferguson tractors to France in the post war years, due mainly to that country's devalued currency. In 1948, for example, only around 1000 tractors were sold in France.

The Standard Motor Company already had an association with Hotchkiss, the French motor manufacturer. A new company, Société Standard-Hotchkiss, was formed to build Ferguson tractors at a new plant on the outskirts of Paris at St. Denis. Sales of these machines were handled by the already established COGEMA which became part of the Ferguson empire and was renamed Harry Ferguson de France.

There was a French connection to the Ferguson story. Using Coventry produced parts, sub assemblies, and engines in the first instance, production did not start until 1953 by which time the merger with Massey Harris meant that the sales company became Compagnie Massey Harris Ferguson. Gradually, reliance on UK built parts declined with engines being sourced from Société Hotchkiss Delahaye.

Not all of the model range produced in the UK were offered. Only the TEA, TEC, TEK, and TEF variants were available initially. The diesel tractors later used French built fuel injection equipment and could be readily identified by the large square Lavalette in line injection pump although some units used Bosch equipment.

By 1956 Massey Ferguson were outstripping Renault in tractor sales on the French domestic market. A change in colour scheme to red chassis and grey bonnet heralded the arrival of the FF-30 series. Unlike UK models, the FF-30 was offered with a petrol engine and in three widths, standard, narrow and vineyard.

Production outgrew the St. Denis factory and in 1958 the Beauvais plant, initially built as a component source for St. Denis, was enlarged. This coincided with the introduction of the French version of the MF-35, the 835, which initially had a Hotchkiss built 23C diesel engine. The St. Denis plant was closed and further new models produced at Beauvais were launched.

Four variants of the 835 were offered, standard, narrow, and vineyard in two widths, along with spark ignition engines for all three types of fuel, petrol, kerosene and lamp oil. The 835 was replaced by the MF-37 in 1959. Another French model was the MF-42 which consisted of an MF-65 rear axle and gearbox fitted with the engine and front end of a MF-37.

The model unique to France, the 20-25, had been developed from the TE-20 fitted with a Perkins 4.99 diesel engine.

The Standard Motor Company had acquired an interest in the tractor market through their links with Ferguson. Once the Banner Lane factory had been sold to Massey Ferguson, it would have seemed logical that Standard should concentrate on car production. The whole idea behind the sale was initially to allow for the expansion necessary to cope with the introduction of the new Triumph Herald car. Relations had not been good between Standard and MF for some time mainly due to the cost of tractor production. MF had been buying Standard shares on the stock market in order to get some influence over the company and eventually acquired over 20% of its share capital. Standard's contract did not expire until 1966, but anxious to obtain funding for expansion of car building, it asked the company for £13 million for Banner Lane. With uncertainty in the air, John Chambers and Trevor Knox, who had worked for Harry Ferguson at Fletchampstead became disillusioned with MF development policy especially the

The first prototype Standard tractor powered by a 23C engine.

influence of Hermann Klemm who had taken over as head of design in the USA in 1945. The pair left and went to work for the Standard Motor Company. Perhaps the loss of the LTX project had been the greatest blow to the Ferguson men. They helped to design a range of tractors for Standard, of which four prototypes are known to have existed, possibly pre-dating the sale of Banner Lane to Massey Ferguson. Standard found that it had a temporary over capacity at its Canley engine works due to MF now using Perkins engines, and to produce its own tractor would have been quite feasible. Trevor Knox had interests in the New Idea Company and it was from this source that implements for the SMC (Standard Motor Company) tractor would come.

The second Standard prototype tractor.

The transmission of the SMC prototypes was innovative with the use of a single gear lever to control all eight forward and two reverse speeds. Immersed disk brakes were also fitted. The two later prototypes had shuttle transmission. The engine was the 23C with separate heater plugs for each cylinder as used in Standard cars.

The acquisition of Standard-Triumph by Leyland Motors in 1961 saw the end of the project. Standard petrol engines continued to be supplied to Massey Ferguson for the few spark ignition 35s and later 135s that were produced and Ford used a Standard

87mm engine in its petrol Dexta. Standard diesel engines similar to those developed for the SMC tractor were also supplied to Allis Chalmers for use in their ED40.

There were also links between Ferguson and eastern Europe. IMT or to give the concern its full title, Industrija Masina Traktora, of Beograd Yugoslavia, started building tractors in the late 1940s. Ferguson designs were adopted and built under licence following an agreement with the Yugoslavian government in 1955 which not only involved the Standard Motor Company but also Frank Perkins Ltd. At that time most of the tractors and equipment were shipped in partly disassembled form and assembled by ITM. As elsewhere, assembly gradually changed to manufacture and ITM merged with the IMR concern who produced the indigenous Zadrugar tractor. The original agreement expired in 1968. From that date, models have generally followed MF designs and the use of Perkins engines has continued. The IMT 539 could be easily identified as being the old MF-35 but larger models were also produced which owe something to the 100 series. Although exports were not allowed originally, by the 1970s IMT tractors were being sold elsewhere, including in the UK. Recent hostilities in the Balkans inflicted severe damage on the IMT factory.

A huge potential market lay in India. Harry Ferguson believed strongly in the benefits of mechanising agriculture in all corners of the globe and the Indian subcontinent was no exception. A newly independent country, India were was keen to mechanise farming and increase food production. Whilst Ferguson set up his own sales organisation in India, the Standard Motor Company, by virtue of its Indian subsidiary Standard Motor Products of India Ltd, handled assembly. In 1960 TAFE was licenced to build MF tractors in India and the Indian version of the MF-35 is now even to be found in the United Kingdom.

The TAFE-35DI assembled in India.

The Italian firm of Landini had roots back into the nineteenth century and produced its first tractors in the 1920s. Single cylinder designs with surface ignition engines were prevalent until 1957 when an agreement was reached with Perkins diesels to build these under licence and install them in a new range of tractors. Following the acquisition of Perkins by MF in 1959, Landini was acquired by them in 1960. During the period covered by this book Landini tractors continued to be built to their own distinctive designs, but certain crawler models were sold in MF colours. Landini also supplied four wheel drive front axles to other MF factories, and in due course certain MF models began to be assembled at the Landini factory.

EBRO in Spain was originally allied to the Ford Motor Company but the Franco government nationalised the concern in 1954. In the 1960s the Fordson Super Major was built using the tooling employed at the the Dagenham plant in England. Then in 1966 agreement was reached with Massey Ferguson and Perkins to build MF tractors. Some strange things happened however, such as the introduction of some strange beasts such as the the EBRO 155, which featured MF 100 series tinwork but underneath was really a Spanish built Fordson Super Major. Once EBRO managed to set its sights on selling tractors abroad, the 100 series tinwork was altered to disguise the MF look and the 155 became the 160E. By fitting Perkins engines the 470 and 684E models were created.

In addition, some MF-100 series tractors were sold in Spain painted blue and silver and badged as EBROs.

The TAFE-35 DI was given a facelift for certain markets to give it almost the appearance of a 100 series tractor.

GLOSSARY

Belt Horsepower – Power measured at the tractor's power take off point. This is usually at a belt pulley attachment but can also be at the PTO (cf).

Bhp – See Horse Power.

Black Tractor – The prototype tractor built in Northern Ireland by Harry Ferguson in 1933.

Brake Horse Power (bhp) – The power developed by an engine under test when attached to a device which measures power under load.

Carcass – The basic tractor before wheels and tinwork are added.

COGEMA – Compagnie Générale du Machinisme Agricole (General Agricultural Machinery Company) France. The French distributor for Ferguson tractors from 1947 to 1952.

Compression Ignition – An engine reliant on a high compression ratio to self ignite the fuel i.e. diesel engine.

Compression Ratio – A measurement achieved by taking the volume of an engine cylinder when at bottom dead centre (at the bottom of its stroke) and at top dead centre (at the top of its stroke). By varying the size of the combustion chamber in the cylinder head high compression can be achieved for fuels like petrol, and low compression for TVO or lamp oil.

Continental Engine Co – A major US supplier of automotive engines.

Conversion Pack – A diesel engine complete with the necessary parts to convert a tractor from its original spark ignition engine to diesel propulsion. Perkins marketed a wide range of conversion packs for most well known makes of tractor. The raison d'etre for the move to diesels in the 1950s was the inconvenience of using two fuels in a TVO powered tractor where one started on petrol, and when warm, changed on to the low cost fuel. TVO often caused performance problems when the tractor was on light work or running too cold.

Depth Wheel – A wheel attached to a plough which can be adjusted in height with relation to the plough body, to set the shares at a certain depth of cut.

Distillate – Similar product to TVO produced in North America.

Double Clutch – A clutch assembly with two driven plates, one to transmit power to the gearbox and the other to the power take off. See also 'live' hydraulics.

Draft Control – The fundamental feature of the Ferguson System whereby a constant depth in work is maintained by the hydraulic system.

Drawbar Horsepower – Power measured at the tractor drawbar on test.

Dry liner – Where the engine cylinder block has the cylinders cast in and is sleeved.

Eastern hemisphere – The sales area consisting of Europe and Asia.

Eros conversion – One of many adaptations to convert the Ford Model T car into a tractor.

Etroit – The French word for narrow.

Greenfield – Village museum near Detroit, Michigan, USA set up by Henry Ford to chart US engineering and social history.

Ground nut scheme – An attempt to encourage the propagation of this plant, a native of South America, as a cash crop, in its African colonies by the British government in the late 1940s. The ground nut is edible and can be used to produce an edible oil. Many machines were bought and exported to Africa to cultivate land in preparation for planting ground nuts including Massey Harris tractors.

Handshake agreement – The name given to an accord between two or more persons where nothing is put in writing

HF Research – Separate company set up by Harry Ferguson to engage in research projects which included four wheel drive for cars and the design of the BMC mini tractor.

Horse power - The power developed by an internal combustion engine calculated basically by the cubic capacity of the engine. See also drawbar horse power, brake horse power and belt horse power.

Lamp oil – Ordinary Kerosene or Paraffin used in some territories as a tractor fuel.

'Live' hydraulics – Where the drive to the hydraulic pump which operates the three point linkage is not broken when the tractor is stopped or put out of gear. This can be achieved by a double clutch (cf) or by driving the hydraulic pump direct from the engine.

LTX – The designation given to the big Ferguson prototypes of the early 1950s.

M-F – Abbreviation for Massey Ferguson.

M-H – Abbreviation for Massey Harris.

Magneto – Self contained device for generating high tension ignition current on an engine.

Mercury V8 – Popular Ford car and truck engine of the 1930s.

Ministry of Supply – The body which controlled all industrial production in the UK during the 1939-45 war.

Multi-Power – Means of doubling the number of gears in a tractor transmission.

NAA – Ford Jubilee tractor built from 1951 to avoid the use of Ferguson patents.

Plow – The American word for a plough. Also used to describe the number of furrows, eg. a two plow tractor would be capable of pulling a two furrow plough.

Position control – An added feature of later M-F tractors whereby the draft control could be locked and an implement held at fixed depth.

Pressure lubrication – The forcing of oil into components of a vehicle engine by means of a pump.

Proprietory – name given to an accessory produced for a motor vehicle by a company other than the manufacturer of the vehicle.

PSV – Public service vehicle such as a bus, tram or trolleybus.

PTO – Power take off. A splined shaft at the rear of the tractor used to power implements by means of a shaft fitted with universal couplings.

Q Cab – A tractor cab incorporating a safety cage and cladding so that the internal noise level is reduced to an acceptable standard.

Rowcrop – The facility to adjust the front and rear tracks of a tractor to allow cultivation along rows of plants without damaging them.

Safety cab - A tractor cab incorporating a safety cage to prevent injury to the driver should the tractor overturn.

Scotch yoke piston. – A simple eccentric device used to drive the pistons in a hydraulic pump.

Shadow factories – Built by the government before the start of the Second World War and used to manufacture munitions and other wartime requirements.

Slipper – An alternative device to a depth wheel.

Spark ignition – An engine reliant on an electric spark to ignite the fuel.

Sump – The base of an internal combustion engine usually used to contain the lubricant.

TE-20 – means Tractor Europe 20HP

Three point linkage – The essential feature of the Ferguson System whereby the implement is attached to the tractor by one top link and two lower links.

TO-20 – means Tractor Overseas 20 HP

Torque convertor – Means of transmitting power from the engine to the rear wheels hydraulically.

TVO – Tractor Vapourising Oil. A hybrid fuel produced during the distillation of crude oil which is not volatile enough to attract excise duty. Specifically produced for agricultural use it had additives to give an octane value of around 60.

Vapouriser – Device for preheating low cost fuels such as TVO, lamp oil or distillate, to allow for their efficient combustion in an internal combustion engine.

Vigneron – French for vineyard.

Vineyard model – A tractor with a narrow track to fit between cultivations such as grape vines, hops or berries.

War Agricultural Committees – The county based bodies which oversaw food production in the United Kingdom during the 1939-45 war. They also licenced the purchase of tractors.

Western Hemisphere – The sales area consisting of the Americas.

Wet liner – Where the engine cylinder bores are separate from the block and fitted in with suitable seals.

We close with a look forward and back with this show scene from the 1970s featuring the 1200 Four Wheel Drive tractor introduced in December 1971 and a selection of historic tractors from the Black Tractor to the Fergie 20, representing the Ferguson legacy. The Massey Harris lineage is represented by the Pacemaker, the Pony and the 4WD.

Massey Ferguson Tractors are still produced at Banner Lane in Coventry, now under the control of AGCO. The machines which are emerging from this historic plant today, will be the stuff of future histories of this great name in the annals of the application of technology to agriculture.

FURTHER READING

Ferguson Implements and Accessories
John Farnworth
Farming Press

Field Guide to Vintage Farm Tractors,
Robert N Pripps,
Voyageur Press.

Ford Farm Tractors,
Randy Leffingwell,
MBI Publishing Company.

Harry Ferguson.
A biography by Colin Fraser.
Old Pond Publications

Massey Harris Album
Allan T Condie
Allan T Condie Publications.

Vintage Tractor Special 1
The Fergie 20 Family, Allan T Condie
Allan T Condie Publications

Vintage Tractor Special 2
Fergie 20, Implements, Accessories and Industrial Equipment. Allan T Condie
Allan T Condie Publications

Vintage Tractor Special 8
Perkins Diesel Conversions.
Allan T Condie
Allan T Condie Publications